A
REASONABLE
FAITH

THE CASE FOR CHRISTIANITY IN
A SECULAR WORLD

A
REASONABLE
FAITH
THE CASE FOR CHRISTIANITY IN A SECULAR WORLD

DR. ANTHONY CAMPOLO

WORD PUBLISHING

Word (UK) Ltd
Milton Keynes, England

WORD BOOKS AUSTRALIA
Heathmont, Victoria, Australia

SUNDAY SCHOOL CENTRE WHOLESALE
Salt River, South Africa

ALBY COMMERCIAL ENTERPRISES PTE LTD
Scotts Road, Singapore

CHRISTIAN MARKETING LTD
Auckland, New Zealand

CROSS (HK) CO
Hong Kong

EUNSUNG CORP
Seoul, Korea

PRAISE INC
Quezon City, Philippines

A REASONABLE FAITH: RESPONDING TO SECULARISM.

ISBN 0-85009-095-4

All Scripture quotations, unless otherwise identified, are from the King James Version of the Bible.

Printed and bound in Great Britain by
Cox and Wyman Ltd,
Reading.

To the priests I meet on
Thursday mornings—

Allen, Craig, and Jim

Acknowledgments

I must thank Anne Gray, Renée Matson, and Kathy Campanella who typed the manuscript for this book, my wife, Peggy, who spent long hours proofreading it, and the editors of Word Books who invited me to write it in the first place. But most of all, I must thank my daughter, Lisa. During the last few years she has become a religion scholar, a thinker, and a critic of theologies. As such, she became a partner in this project. She edited what I wrote, challenged what I thought, argued with my convictions, and refused to let me write anything that I did not really believe. She helped me rewrite large sections of this book, stayed up nights trying to figure out better ways for me to express difficult ideas, and made writing this book a lot of fun for me.

Contents

A Preliminary Note from the Author

A friend of mine was a missionary in Burma. One day while he was standing on a street corner preaching the Gospel, a hostile crowd gathered around him. They tried to shout him down and constantly interrupted his message with catcalls. Vainly he struggled to deliver his sermon, but the sentiment of the crowd was too much against him. Just as he was ready to give up a Buddhist monk came by. The monk silenced the crowd with a loud cry and then he said, "Listen to this man. Don't you know *he needs* to tell you about his God?"

What an interesting observation. The Buddhist monk was sensitive to the fact that my friend *needed* to preach his sermon more than the crowd needed to hear it. I am sure that this is the case with what I have to share in this book. I do not know how much others need what I have to say but I know that I *need* to say it.

I spent ten years of my life teaching at a large Ivy League university. During that time I tried to share my Christian convictions with secularists and agnostics. From my discussions with them I learned a great deal. Most of all I learned which approaches for communicating the Gospel were appreciated by my cultured colleagues and which elicited negative responses. I learned which arguments challenged my listeners and which were brushed aside as meaningless. Little by little I developed a style for expressing my faith in a way that seemed credible to them. Out of these experiences came the need to draw my arguments together and to try to unify them into a single systematized presentation. *I needed* to organize my various arguments so that I could see how they fit together to make my case for the Christian faith.

It seemed that many of my secularist friends were viewing Christianity as a naïve mythology that defied reason and required of its believers a schizophrenic mentality. They knew there were intellectuals who were Christians, but they tended to think that such Christians compartmentalized their thinking and held their religious beliefs totally apart from their academic disciplines. They tended to view us as persons who had one mind-set while performing our intellectual tasks and another mind-set for being religious.

I wanted them to realize that such assumptions about Christians were wrong; that most of us worked hard at integrating our academic knowledge with our religious convictions. I wanted them to realize that we did not hold a set of beliefs that flew in the face of reason, even if reason alone could not make them into believers. I wanted them to recognize Christianity as a viable option for understanding the world, even if they themselves could not buy into it. Furthermore, I wanted my secularist friends to realize that many of their own ideas and discoveries had religious implications. I wanted them to see that religion was more a part of their world than they might imagine. I believed that with prodding and encouragement they might see that many of the discoveries of science and insights of contemporary philosophy could be signposts that pointed to God. In the midst of thinking limited by logic and empiricism, there are, in the words of Peter Berger, "rumors of angels."

I also had a need to defend my secular friends before the Christian community. In so many ways the discussions about secular humanists which I had heard in Christian circles convinced me that the Christians had many misconceptions about who and what secularists are and what they believe. Too often Christians have assumed that secular humanists are joyless, unfulfilled people writhing in the despair of meaningless existence; that they are people restlessly seeking an escape from an inner, agonizing emptiness.

For better or for worse I have not found them to be so. Oh, there are the expected neurotics and malcontents among them, but for the most part they are very much like the people I have met in churches. Most of them have a commitment to social justice, an appreciation of the worth and dignity of human beings, a compassion for the poor and oppressed, and a desire to enhance their own humanness. They are good people who seem to be gaining a certain sense of fulfillment from their work and who seem to be enjoying life. After getting to know them well, I have become convinced that they too need Jesus, often for reasons which they do not fully understand. But secularists are generally happy people.

Some Christians view secular humanists as agents of the Antichrist who are out to destroy the church with their godless philosophies. Some even see them as agents of some kind of subtle communist plot to weaken the religious foundations of America, rendering us defenseless against a Russian takeover. I almost hate to minimize this drama, but I find secularists to be generally tolerant people.

I need for my Christian friends to realize that "humanism" is not necessarily a bad word. If secularists mean by humanism that man is the measure of all things and the creator of all values, then of course Christians must be the enemies of humanism. But if they mean by humanism the desire to see every person actualize his/her highest potential, grow into peaceful, self-giving, loving persons, and build oneness among all the peoples of the world, then humanism shares much with Christianity. Furthermore, I desperately need to show my secularist friends that if they adhere to this latter concept of humanism, then Jesus provides the answer to achieving their aspirations for the human race. Indeed, there is such a thing as Christian humanism. It is held by those who believe that Jesus came into the world, not simply to provide a way to heaven, but to show all the people of the world how they could become fully human and live life more abundantly. I believe that Jesus not only incarnates God but that he also incarnates the fullness of humanity. Consequently, Jesus is the ultimate expression of what humanists want every one of us to become.

We Christians need not be at war with the humanists of this latter stripe. As a matter of fact, we have a lot to talk about, particularly since we Christians believe that we know the only way in which humanistic goals can be realized.

Most of my secularist friends call themselves "existentialists." Unfortunately, the very mention of the word *existentialism* runs shudders up and down the spines of many evangelicals. To many Christians, existentialism is a godless philosophy that is devoid of absolute values and holds to no truth beyond human experience. Indeed, there are existentialist philosphers, such as Jean-Paul Sartre and Friedrich Nietzsche, who might to some degree approximate such a caricature. However, there is also a long line of religious existentialists such as Martin Buber, Jacques Maritain, Nicolas Berdayev and Søren Kierkegaard. These latter representatives of the existentialist movement have written some of the most meaningful religious literature of our time.

Existentialism is not a philosophy; *it is a method* of establishing truth in the mind of man. That method is basically through commitment. Consequently, every Christian is a kind of existentialist. When a secularist student asks me why I believe the Bible, I answer, "Because I decided to." Then I ask, "Why is it that you do *not* believe the Bible?" The student usually thinks over the question and answers, "I guess because I decided *not* to."

Reason and arguments can build up a case for or against the Bible and the existence of God, but finally each of us must make a personal decision. Even after Christianity is viewed as a reasonable faith, the individual still must make what Søren Kierkegaard called "a leap of faith." That leap may be made on the basis of thoughtful arguments and after all other options have been reasonably explored. But ultimately a decision must be made, a commitment must take place, and a person must realize what Blaise Pascal knew: "The heart has reason which reason can never know."

I also need for my Christian friends to know that science is not an enemy of Christianity. The discoveries of the great women and men who have researched the wonders of nature do not offer an alternate system of truth to Christian beliefs. Their knowledge is part of that one system of truth which glorifies God. I myself have found that science—in my case social science—does not destroy my Christian faith but helps me to understand it more fully. I want my Christian friends to overcome feelings of intellectual inferiority, come out of hiding, and enter into discussion with people in science. Not only will Christians learn much that will deepen them as Christians, but they will be able to contribute much to the way in which people of science view the world.

Jesus once said that the Kingdom of God is like "a householder which bringeth forth out of his treasure things new and old" (Matt. 13:52).

So it is for all who want to integrate faith and knowledge. There are a number of old things we cherish: our faith in God; our belief in an afterlife; our hope for the future of the world; our belief in absolutes for living; the conviction that each of us is infinitely precious and can have a meaningful existence.

There are many new things being discovered each day: that our images of God are creations of the collective imagination of our society; that the arms race between the U.S. and the U.S.S.R. is out of control; that history is a class struggle between the oppressed peoples of the world and their oppressors; that each of us is required to create meaning for life in the midst of existence. There is a need to put the old beliefs and the new discoveries together in some kind of harmonious fashion. It is a need that I have and I want to share my efforts to meet this need with all who may have a similar need.

I
WHAT IS SECULARISM?

1.
The End of the Magical Kingdom

When my son was a boy I asked him if he knew what it meant to have faith. He quickly responded by saying, "Faith is believing what I know isn't true."

That simple statement more and more characterizes how many secularized thinkers view the maintenance of a religious belief system in today's world. They contend that holding to religious faith requires going far beyond what it is intellectually possible to accept without being dishonest. It is not that they do not want to believe in God and Christian doctrine. Quite the contrary; they often desperately want to believe in such things. But they have been reared in a culture where believing in spiritual realities which transcend the boundaries of logic and empirical verification proves very difficult.

As a faculty member at a large Ivy League university, I was confronted in my office one day by a young woman who was a graduate student in chemistry. She was weeping and on the verge of total emotional collapse. Some of her colleagues had tried to help her out of her distress by taking her to the mental health clinic of the university, and, when that failed, they decided to take her to a man they jokingly referred to as "the resident believer." They figured that if "scientific" help had failed to comfort her, maybe religion should be tried as a last resort. They were not religious themselves but were pragmatic enough to know that, whether it was fact or fiction, religion sometimes "worked" in such cases.

The young woman had been engaged to be married to a student at Columbia University, an institution about ninety miles away from our school. They had been carrying on a telephone conversation in the late evening a few days earlier. The talk had become increasingly amorous until her fiancé announced that he was going to hang up the telephone and drive over to see her immediately. He claimed that he *had* to see her and be with her. While driving on the New Jersey turnpike, he fell asleep at the wheel of his car, swerved the vehicle under the wheels of a tractor-trailer, and was killed instantly.

On the day of the funeral, when she entered the funeral home, the young woman was confronted by her dead lover's hysterical mother who pointed at her accusingly and screamed, "If it had not been for you, my boy would be alive today."

The guilt and sorrow became more than the young woman could bear. She collapsed, and, when she was revived, entered into such a state of melancholia that she did not care whether she lived or died. I tried my best to comfort her, using Scripture. I explained to her that Jesus had died to provide forgiveness and that He was spiritually present to deliver her from guilt, to give her hope, and to give new direction to her life. All the right arguments were used. C. S. Lewis would have been proud of me. But it was all to no avail. She cried out in desperation, "I want to believe you. Don't you understand that? You don't have to convince me that I *should* become a Christian believer. I want that more than anything right now—it would solve all of my problems. But I can't *make* myself believe it. It doesn't ring with truth for me. Oh, how I wish it did, but it doesn't."

I thought of the man who brought his son to Jesus for healing and was told that it was possible for the boy to be healed if only the man would believe. The man cried out, "Lord, I believe; help my unbelief."

This graduate student desperately wanted help for her unbelief. She wanted to find a way to believe something that in the modern world no longer seemed believable. George Santayana once said of the modern secularist that he does not reject God, but sadly bids Him a fond farewell. So it was with this woman. The possibility of God had slipped out of the perception of reality into which she had been socialized. She was no reprobate atheist. She was a desperate woman who wanted to believe—but couldn't.

THE DEVELOPMENT OF THE SECULAR MIND

How did it happen that we creatures, whom some have considered to be incurably religious, have come into a time when God is not so much rejected as relegated to being an antiquated irrelevancy? What events have led us into a world-view that seems to require no reference to divine revelations to explain the natural universe or to give purpose to human existence? How has it become possible to maintain order in a societal system that no longer requires theological legitimations for its norms and laws? The founder of modern sociology, Auguste Comte, tried to answer these questions. He claimed to have discovered the law of unilinear evolution which governed humanity's intellectual development. While more empirically oriented successors demonstrated that Comte's thinking lacked the kind of verification which establishes natural laws, there can be little doubt that he provided a good description of the history of intellectual constructions of reality, from society's beginnings to our present state.

Comte taught that our society evolved through two stages of

thinking on its way to the present positivistic secular form. The two earlier stages of evolutionary development are the theological stage and the metaphysical stage.[1]

The Theological Stage of Thinking

In its earliest phase, according to Comte, society employed theology to explain all elements of reality and to legitimate all its social institutions. All knowledge was deduced from religious assumptions. God was believed to be the creator of both the heavens and earth. All mores and folkways were viewed as having divine origins. All academic disciplines were steeped in religio-magical thinking. Before chemistry there was alchemy; before mathematics there was numerology. According to Comte, religious assumptions were a priori to all kinds of thinking and explanation.

Political leaders learned to utilize religious explanations of societal systems to their advantage. They were well aware that if the populace believed their right to rule originated in "the will of God," their positions of power would be significantly strengthened. From ancient times to the French Revolution, people were encouraged to believe in the divine right of kings. If they believed that God ordained their king and the structure of the governing system, people were less likely to rebel against their ruler and his government, regardless of how oppressive such government might be.

Karl Marx was well aware of the results that occur when rulers legitimate their socioeconomic systems with religion. He clearly noted the cynicism of the ruling class which propagated religion as a means for buttressing its position of privilege. Religion made a rebellion of the proletariat against its oppressors into a rebellion against the will of God, and thus aided the ruling classes in their efforts to stay in power. Marx justifiably pointed out that religion so used becomes an instrument of oppression. If religion leads people to believe that oppressive rulers are ordained of God, then it rightly deserves all the ridicule and scorn heaped upon it by its critics.[2]

Surprisingly, many contemporary Christians still hold to doctrines of the divine right of rulers and condemn all forms of civil disobedience. Quoting the thirteenth chapter of the Epistle to the Romans, they insist that any opposition to government, regardless of its tyrannical character, is resistance to the will of God:

> Let every soul be subject unto the higher powers. For there is no power but of God: the powers that be are ordained of God. Whosoever therefore resisteth the power, resisteth the ordinance of God: and they that resist shall receive to themselves damnation. For rulers are not a terror to good works, but to the evil. Wilt thou then not be afraid of the power? Do that which is good, and thou shalt have praise of the same: For he is the minister of God to thee for good. But if thou do that which is evil, be afraid: for he beareth not the sword in vain: for he is the minister of God, a revenger to execute wrath upon him that doeth evil.
>
> *Romans 13:1–4*

It is interesting to note that this dogma and Scripture were used by church leaders in Nazi Germany to justify their failure to challenge Hitler. They argued that to rebel against his dictatorship, regardless of how evil it proved to be, would be contrary to the requisites of Scripture. More recently in the United States, the Bill Gothard Youth Conflict Seminars have propagated ideas that verge on the same kind of thinking. Gothard teaches that there is a divinely ordained "chain of command." Each level of that chain is responsible to obey the one directly above it. If those who are in positions of superordination do wrong, the subordinates are still required to be obedient. God will judge the superordinates if they govern wrongly; the subordinates will be judged on the basis of their obedience to those who are above them and not according to the social consequences which might result from supporting such leaders.

There was a time when I held such views, and I can remember distinctly the circumstances which brought about a change in my thinking. I was conducting a series of lectures at a southern college as part of that school's Religious Emphasis Week when my ideas concerning civil disobedience were challenged and changed. At the conclusion of one of my lectures, I opened up the meeting for questions from the floor. One young man who spoke in a heavy southern drawl addressed a question to me. Those of us who hail from the American northeast have a tendency to be prejudiced against people who speak that way, assuming them to be lacking in intellectual sophistication. Thus, we are unprepared to defend ourselves against such persons if they come up with brilliant arguments against our positions. Such was the case in my encounter with this unsuspected intellectual. He simply asked, "What's your opinion of civil disobedience?"

The question was particularly relevant at the time. It was during the height of the Civil Rights Movement, and Martin Luther King had just practiced civil disobedience, been arrested, and published his eloquent *Letter From the Birmingham Jail*. Indifferent to the implications of these events, I arrogantly dismissed his question by quoting the passage from Romans cited above. Then I asked, "Does that answer your question?"

"Not exactly," he responded in that southern accent. "Where was the Apostle Paul when he wrote that stuff?" he asked in his slow, drawn-out fashion.

Somewhat embarrassed, I had to say, "In jail."

"How did he get there?" asked my young inquisitor.

Before I could answer he said, "Let me tell you. They were havin' racial problems in the church down there in Jerusalem. The Jews and the Gentiles weren't gettin' along too well. They had separate churches and all that kind of stuff. So the apostles decided they'd get together to work out the problem. Paul not only decided to go to that meeting, but he decided to take a Gentile with him—you can read about it in the Book of Acts.

Now people from those two races didn't travel together in them days. It was against the Jewish law, but Paul didn't seem to care about them Jewish laws. I don't know what you call that, but it sounds like the first 'Freedom Ride' to me.

"When they got to Jerusalem they ate together in a place where people could see them. Now, that may not seem to be much to you, mister, but they were breakin' the rules of that segregated Jewish society, that didn't allow for Jews and Gentiles to eat together like that. I don't know what you call that, but it sounds like the first 'sit-in' to me.

"Then they headed down to the temple. Paul was goin' to violate the rules of the Jews and take that man from the other race right into the holy place where only Jewish men could pray. Ya see, they had segregated churches in them days. That was too much for the crowd. It's one thing to have a 'Freedom Ride,' and it's another to have a 'sit-in,' but Paul and his friend from the other race was about to stage a 'pray-in.' Imagine, Paul just kept on breakin' the rules of the rulers.

"Then the crowd rioted. They started beatin' on Paul and his friend. So the Roman police had to come, and they took the two of them into 'protective custody.' When they got those boys down to the jail house, they practiced a little 'police brutality.' The next day Paul told them jailers they picked on the wrong guys, 'cause Paul was a Roman citizen, and they had violated his civil rights.

"Those policemen were scared and tried to settle out of court, but Paul appealed to the Supreme Court for a rulin'. Now, in those days the Supreme Court was in Rome. It was on his way to Rome that Paul wrote that stuff you just read. How come a man in jail who has broken so many of the rules written up by kings and potentates would write what you just read? How could Paul, of all people, be against civil disobedience?"

Needless to say, I was humbled and put in my proper place. I realized that things were not as simple as I had made them appear with a proof-text to support my case. I still believe that God wants us all "to be subject to the higher powers," but being subject to these powers does not always mean to obey them. The rulers always offer *two* alternatives to the Christian—obey or be punished. There come times when, like the leaders of the New Testament church, the Christian must say, "I must obey God rather than man."

However, when the Christian feels that he must disobey the leaders of the state, he must present himself to accept the second alternative and voluntarily surrender to the punishment that the state hands out to its nonconformists. This is why Martin Luther King did not avoid arrest when he broke the Jim Crow laws of Alabama. On the one hand, his civil disobedience exposed the immorality of the state in perpetuating those laws. On the other hand, he upheld the authority of government by submitting to arrest and punishment. He was "subject to the higher powers" even when his Christian conscience compelled him to disobey the dictates of those powers.

This is why I believe that it was wrong for Christians who were opposed to the Vietnam War to flee from the United States to Canada. I believe they were right in refusing to participate in the insane killing of that conflict, but they should have offered themselves for arrest rather than trying to evade the authority of the state. Of course, it is easy for me to say these things since I was too old to be existentially involved in draft resistance. However, I still believe that the principle is biblically sound and pragmatically effective.

Perhaps if the tens of thousands of war resisters had offered themselves for arrest, Americans would have been forced to ask the kind of questions that could have resulted in national repentance. If they had been willing to have been "persecuted for righteousness' sake," Americans might have responded differently to their refusal to fight in Vietnam. I do not believe that violent rebellions are the only way to resist sinful and oppressive regimes. I contend that nonconformity to evil systems even to the point of punishment by death can effectively challenge unjust rulers and bring about change. The resurrection of Jesus vindicated crucifixion as the ultimate means of challenging the "principalities and powers and rulers of this age." The world is still waiting to be challenged by people who are willing to be crucified for the causes of God.

In addition to political utilizations, theological legitimation is used to support all social norms, roles, and meanings for life. The poor farmer is told that God ordained him to be born to his role and lot in life. The economic arrangements that facilitate the exploitation of workers while the owners of the means of production gain disproportionate and exorbitantly unfair profits are deemed part of a divine plan.

The Metaphysical Stage of Thinking

When men and women seek the meaning of existence or try to create their own destinies, they are told by propagators of religious thought that all of these things have been decided for them before the foundation of the world. They are informed that they are called to submit to an essential meaning for life which precedes their existence in time and space. To do otherwise would be disobedience to their "heavenly calling." Jean Paul Sartre calls such behavior an exercise in "bad faith." To assume that people are not free to participate in making those decisions which determine their individual destinies is to deny them their humanity, says Sartre. Consequently, he lauds the collapse of the theological stage of thinking with its accompanying tyranny and terror.

Historically, the theological stage of societal evolution was dealt a death blow by the French Revolution and the beheading of King Louis. In one dramatic act the ancient regime and its religiously sanctioned order came to an end. While Frenchmen stood in awed silence, the guillotine slid down its course—the people had defied the "divinely ordained" ruler. They were now themselves in charge of society. They had usurped the responsibilities of writing the laws, establishing order, and charging their collective and individual destinies. They were in desperate need of some new basis for societal norms and regulations. To serve as guidelines for their brave new world they needed some principles that transcended individual whims and wishes. To replace the theological orientation of their abandoned past they required a new world-view, and fortunately, they had the philosophers of the Enlightenment.

Jean-Jacques Rousseau, the Marquis de Condorcet, Louis Bonald, and hosts of other intellectuals had produced an abundance of literary works and ideas that served as the foundation of the second stage of societal evolution—the metaphysical stage. These heralds of a new age arrived just in time to re-define nature and society without reference to theological postulates. Henceforth, the natural universe would no longer be viewed merely as a creation of God upheld and governed by His will. Instead it would be viewed as a vast and complex machine governed by its own inherent rationale and laws. The philosophers of the Enlightenment suggested that it remained for rational man to explore his universe, to discover the laws that ruled its movements and the principles which were operative in its structure.[3]

The human mind was assumed to be capable of mastering this knowledge, and of using it to provide the basis for restructuring society along the rational lines of the universal laws of nature. A new social order would be established, in harmony with the laws of nature rather than the laws of God. Humanity was believed to have been perverted by the erroneous patterns established by the old religious society. In this new metaphysical stage described by Comte, the religious world-view would be discarded and the mind of man would direct society into a rational and perfected natural order. The philosophers of the Enlightenment glorified the innate capacity of man and gave birth to an optimism about the future of the human race, now freed from the superstitions and limitations of the religious past.

Despite the fact that because of their aristocratic heritage many of these philosophers were put to death by the rabble of the revolution, they continued to believe until the bitter end that man's rational understanding would ultimately pave the way for a new and better age. The Marquis de Condorcet wrote his great work *Progress of the Human Mind* while in prison awaiting his turn for the guillotine. He faced death with the assurance that a utopian era was about to dawn.

This metaphysical stage was one that gave rise to democracy. Only those who believe in the capacity of common men to chart rationally the most favorable course for societal progress could will for them the power to determine their own destinies and the future of their nations. Only a confidence in the innate goodness of man would lead to a form of government that trusted men, rather than God, to establish laws for behavior. In the rhetoric of U.S. nationalism it is popular to say that our nation was born out of Christian teachings, but the doctrine of original sin, such a powerful influence on our Calvinistic forebears, hardly provides grounds for trusting the masses with moral decision-making. If people are as sinful as those stern Puritans suggested, they are hardly to be entrusted with the reins of power. We must credit the philosophers of the Enlightenment with the liberal view that men, freed from the negative restraints of religion, have the reason and moral capacity to create "a more perfect form of government."

Looking back on the thinking of the Enlightenment which characterized the Comtean metaphysical stage of societal evolution, we cannot help being impressed with its naïveté. What is even more surprising is that there are still pseudosophisticates who believe these things today and who scoff at religion and the social order it prescribes as a cause of prejudice, hatred, and destructive tyrannical power. I cannot help wondering how many world wars, holocausts, nuclear explosions and communist dictatorships it will take to convince these seemingly incurable optimists that there is an irrational quality to human nature which expresses itself in behavior that is desperately wicked. A religious mind-set is not required to reach this conclusion about human beings. Quite to the contrary, devastating arguments against the optimistic ideology of human nature are mounted by some of the most severe critics of religion.

Freud set forth a revelation about human nature that sent shock waves through the hopeful, idealistic intellectual milieu of neo-Hegelian Europe and the haughty arrogance of the English Victorians. He broke with the romantic conceptions of human nature expressed in the art and literature of the times by exploring the depths of the human psyche. There he found insatiable sexual lusts, and cravings for libidinal pleasures which knew no bounds. He discovered that behavior was more powered by the irrational impulses of the *id* than by the societally trained *superego*.[4]

Furthermore, Freud discovered a terrible death wish suppressed in the subconscious of each individual. He argued that when we realize that sexual cravings cannot be fully gratified, we seek a reduction of our sexual tensions through the cessation of life, thereby finally and completely removing ourselves from the insurmountable obstacles to our pleasure. But there is something even more perverse than this at the root of human nature. Freud talks of a deadly destructive force called *Thanatos* in almost the same manner that the Apostle Paul talks about "the law of sin and death" in the Epistle to the Romans. He sees a force at work in the human psyche that struggles against *Eros*, the dynamic creative energy of man. Like a high priest in the Homeric age, he seems to implore the forces of Eros to rise up against the forces of Thanatos that seem to be sweeping through history and moving us toward an inevitable entropic state, but he doubts the power of Eros to overcome the awesome threat of Thanatos. Freud hardly holds to the positive hope of the philosophers of the metaphysical stage.[5]

Friedrich Nietzsche saw that the "death of the gods" did not lead into an era of tenderness, reason, and peace. Rather, Nietzsche rejoiced that the true nature of man would be revealed in the "will to power." Without gods, he believed, man would realize that his true destiny was to transcend himself and become the superman. This could only happen by a "transvaluation of ethics" which would lead man "beyond good and evil." Nietzsche celebrated and glorified this tendency toward prideful assertion of self against the constraints of society, which he referred to as "the herd." He showed that the vision of rational perfection so dearly embraced by the philosophers of the Enlightenment had no basis in the nature of man. The metaphysical stage was propelled by the lingering effects of religion, but the effects of this residue of religion were to be short-lived. It was an era rightly described as the "twilight of the gods."[6]

Some of the more recent interpretations of what it means to be human leave us still more depressed about our natural condition. Erving Goffman describes us as actors presenting images of who we are to those we meet for the purpose of "conning" them. He says we present ourselves to others in ways that will convince them that we have qualities and traits worth admiring and loving, when in reality we may not possess those qualities at all. In his brilliant book *The Presentation of Self in Everyday Life*, he leaves us stripped of any dignity by illustrating the ways in which we play dramatic roles that conceal who we really are. But worse than that, he leaves us with the suggestion that beneath all of the manipulative roles, there might not be any essential self at all. We suffer the grim realization that we are nothing more than the sum total of all the phony con jobs we have pulled off in our social interactions.[7]

The optimism of the French Republic came to an end historically with Napoleon. Democracy ended in a dictatorship more totalitarian than the reign of absolute monarchs. At least the kings of the ancient regime faced countervailing powers in the clergy, the aristocracy, and the guilds. The Napoleonic dictators swept away these controlling power blocks and established a rule that answered to no one—especially not to the God who had been expelled from political thought and structure. In the theological stage, those who rebelled against their rulers were considered to be enemies of God. By the end of the short-lived metaphysical stage, those who rebelled against their leaders were considered to be enemies of the people. Supposedly, the new rulers ruled by the will of the people, according to the laws established by the people and for the people. It is certain that the wrath of "the people" was often more tyrannical than the wrath of "God" which fell on those of an earlier time.

The Positivistic Stage of Thinking

Comte saw the societal collapse that accompanied the end of the metaphysical stage but he did not despair. His optimism would not be stifled by the tragedies surrounding him. He believed that the human race was about to enter a utopian era which would transcend the obstructions of the metaphysical philosophers and construct a new society on the basis of science. He called this third and final stage in the development of human thought "the positivistic stage." In this stage, empirical facts and logic would suggest the structure of society and the moral codes by which men and women should govern their lives. It was to this end that Comte began to develop a new science called sociology.

Comte hoped the practitioners of this new science would carry out empirical studies that would provide the knowledge of what norms, societal structures, and economic practices would deliver the most good to the greatest number. His sociology was hardly "value-free," as some of his successors in this field have argued it should be. For him, sociology was a scientific tool which would be used to build a society on the conclusions of science.

Comte believed that the priests of the Christian Church should be replaced by a new breed of moral teachers. These new clerics would articulate a morality based on positivism and would empirically demonstrate the validity of every doctrine they taught. Comte outlined how this new clerical order should be organized, even to the point of setting forth the qualities of its chief potentate—a pope of positivism. Not surprising, if one knows something of the character of Comte, he thought that he alone had the qualities to hold this lofty position.

Comte's proposals for a positivistic religion were never attempted and his perfected society has not begun to be realized, but his prediction that the thinking of humanity would become increasingly positivistic has indeed come to pass. In the thought processes of modern men and women, logic and empiricism increasingly determine what is meaningful and acceptable. Anything that cannot be apprehended with the senses or be subjected to logical calculations is hard for those who are socialized into the modern canons of thought.

While the evolutionary process into the positivistic stage is not complete in every area of human endeavor and while all persons are not imbued with a positivistic mind-set, there is ample evidence that the unilinear progression toward positivism is everywhere at work. For example, a survey of changes in beliefs and attitudes towards homosexuality clearly demonstrates the movement from theological thinking to positivistic thinking.

In the first stage, homosexual behavior was considered immoral because it violated the will of God, and homosexuals were seen as ungodly. As society moved into the metaphysical stage, homosexual behavior came to be viewed as contrary to the laws of nature, and the homosexual was considered out of harmony with the natural ways for humans to behave. Homosexual acts were viewed as "unnatural" and they were thus referred to in the laws of this country, many of which were written in the eighteenth century. As we move into the positivistic stage, however, empirical research has led most social scientists to believe that homosexuality is not necessarily the result of the overly lascivious and lustful behavior of insatiable sexual appetites, as is set forth in the first chapter of

Romans. Furthermore, there is growing evidence that the sexual orientation of the homosexual results from his or her bio-
physical make-up. In view of new research to support such
claims, many lawmakers now view homosexual behavior as
being in harmony with the physiological nature of the homosexual person and therefore not to be considered unnatural. A
positivistic approach to homosexual behavior has led, consequently, to a move toward liberalization.

I do not wish to become embroiled in the legal arguments of
this issue; I simply want to point out that positivistic thinking
is increasingly evident in the discussion of such matters and is
exerting a determining influence on how we view things.
When I talk about the will of God in such matters or explain
that there are biblical principles that should guide us in such
things as our socioeconomic activities, I am not so much
ridiculed as viewed as a curiosity from another age, that has
somehow survived into the modern era. My very existence
seems to belie the fact that my kind of theological orientation
should have long ago become extinct.

Antony Flew tells a wonderful story to demonstrate the
positivistic approach to things. His story demonstrates that
this style of thinking does not refute the existence of God (no
empirical evidence could ever be mustered to do such a thing)
but rather relegates "God talk" to the realm of irrelevancy.

Once upon a time two explorers came upon a clearing in the jungle.
In the clearing were growing many flowers and many weeds. One
explorer says, "Some gardener must tend this plot." The other dis-
agrees. "There is no gardener." So they pitch their tents and set a
watch. No gardener is ever seen. "But perhaps he is an invisible
gardener." So they set up a barbed wire fence. They electrify it.
They patrol with bloodhounds. . . . But no shrieks ever suggest that
some intruder has received a shock. No movement of the wire ever
betrays an invisible climber. The bloodhounds never give cry. Yet
still the Believer is not convinced. "But there is a gardener, invisible, intangible, insensible to electric shocks, a gardener who has no
scent and makes no sound, a gardener who comes secretly to look
after the garden which he loves." At last the Sceptic despairs. "But

what is left of your original assertion? Just how does what you call an invisible, intangible, eternally elusive gardener differ from an imaginary gardener or even from no gardener at all?"

Flew concludes, "A fine brash hypothesis may thus be killed by inches, the death of a thousand qualifications."[8]

2.
When Secularity Replaces Religion

Emile Durkheim correctly pointed out that a description is not an explanation. We have used the theories of Auguste Comte to describe the development of Western thinking, which moved in a unilinear fashion away from "God talk" to positivism. However, to explain why this progression took place, it is helpful to turn to Max Weber, another of the founding fathers of sociology.

THE INCREASING TENDENCY TO RATIONALIZATION

Weber observed that in all areas of behavior and social organization, there is an increasing tendency for people to seek rational ways of acting and explaining things. Like Comte, he saw that during the earliest stages of intellectual and social development, people tried to make sense out of reality by religious explanations. Prior to logical or scientific explanations for the behavioral expectations of society, the working of nature, and the meaning of catastrophes and illness, it is likely that people will resort to religious myth or magic.

When primitive children ask why there are certain rules that limit their freedom, their parents might tell them that their god established these rules. When the children ask why there is thunder and lightning, they might be told that God is angry. If illness overtakes a member of a tribe, it might be an accepted belief that the individual is demon-possessed. However, the religio-magical constructions of reality are doomed to extinction in most societies, as, little by little, observations and discoveries lead people to realize that there are also scientific explanations for things.

With a scientific understanding of the world, rules exist because they meet the functional requisites of the society. Thunder and lightning come to be explained as the result of a buildup of static electricity in the clouds, and illness is discovered to have natural physical and mental causes.

There is a steady encroachment of rational-scientific explanation into the world-view of any society. As this happens, people gradually turn away from religious authorities in seeking answers to questions about the origin and nature of their world and society. Weber argues that nothing can stop this process, which he calls "the increasing tendency toward rationalization."[1]

The Economic Implications of Rationalization

This tendency toward rationalization is most likely to take effect first in economics. As a primitive people struggle for survival in a world of limited resources, they tend to seek the most efficient means of providing themselves with the food, clothing, and shelter necessary for survival. The most efficient way for them to support themselves requires a scientific approach to production. For instance, if empirical evidence demonstrates that growing a crop in a certain way produces a greater yield per acre than the religiously prescribed manner, the religious way will eventually be replaced by the new method. Religious institutions may exercise restraints on scientific innovations, but history attests that these restraints seldom succeed very long.

The inclination to accept scientifically prescribed, efficient means of production is accelerated if the society is in competition with other societies. Usually, efficiency in production can give a society an edge over its competitors.

Once a scientific method of improving the way people carry out basic economic activities is introduced to a society, it is the beginning of the end of their religious world-view. The rational scientific approach to doing things soon spreads into all areas of life. People look for the most efficient ways to heal the sick, teach the young, organize government activities, render social services, and even carry out their religious activities. In recent times, there is evidence that Christian denominations are structured more in accord with the organizing principles of businesses and bureaucracies than by a pattern perceived as divinely ordained. After all, in a pluralistic society, it is the most efficiently organized denomination which is able to "win out" against its "competitors." In such a social system, everything is understood and organized along rational-scientific lines.

Explaining the Unexplainable

There are those religionists who argue against this viewpoint and point out that there are crucial gaps in man's scientific knowledge that must still be filled with religious explanations. They contend that science cannot tell us much about the origin of the physical universe, the creation of life, and human mind-body relationships. These, and a host of other critical problems concerning our lives and the meaning of our existence, seem to evade resolution via the scientific method.

Some scientists have agreed with this claim of religious apologists. The Heisenberg theory of indeterminacy demonstrates how a deficiency in scientific understanding forces man back upon religious explanations. Some scientists argue that this theory implies a transscientific explanation for atomic and molecular structures. According to Werner Karl Heisenberg, an electron can assume a variety of orbits around the nucleus of the atom, and there are no known natural laws governing which orbit is taken. It is as though the electrons "willed" or freely "chose" their paths of movement, with no regard to determinants such as influence other natural processes. Furthermore, there is good evidence to suggest that there is no possibility that any natural explanation for the orbital movements of electrons can be discovered. It is easy for the religiously inclined to conclude that God governs these movements in ways that are "past finding out."

Karl Heim, a twentieth-century German theologian, finds religious implications in the fourth dimension of the universe postulated by Einstein. Heim suggests that the fourth dimension gives evidence of a reality that transcends time, space, and matter, as we know it.[2]

I am not so sure that Heisenberg's electrons or Einstein's fourth dimension will always be beyond the scope of positivistic scientific knowledge. What is beyond human understanding today is often within our grasp tomorrow. Quite often the "inexplicable" ends up being explained. Thus, while secularists readily admit that there are gaps in human knowledge which are easily filled with religious explanations, they contend that these gaps will eventually be eliminated when science is more fully developed. Such "missing links," according to secularists, are only a condition of science's relative newness as the basis for the explanation of all reality. Future research and study will drive out the last ghost from our spirit-infested world and lead to a completely rational understanding of ourselves and our universe.

I recently heard a preacher brilliantly argue that the stories of the Bible could be reconciled with modern science. He stressed that there is nothing in Scripture that contradicts the

laws of science. He pointed out that even the miracles were
possible within the parameters of scientific thinking.

What this well-meaning preacher unwittingly did was to
testify to the triumph of scientific thinking in his own mind.
Rather than contending that science was true because it
agreed with the Bible, he argued that the Bible was true because it could be reconciled with science. For this clergyman,
science had become the ultimate authority. His modern
world-view allowed only for truth as defined by positivism.

The Influence of the Reformers

In tracing the historical development of the increasing tendency towards rationalization in Western societies, Max
Weber gives special attention to the influence of Protestantism. He recognized that the theologians who gave birth to the
Reformation initiated a movement that would demythologize
Christianity. The superstitious, magical practices and the
mythical folklore that had developed and become intertwined
with Christian theology would be systematically destroyed
under the sway of Martin Luther, John Calvin, Huldreich
Zwingli, and their successors. The ritual of Holy Mass would
lose its miraculousness and become of principally symbolic
value; the saints would lose the magical quality they held for
many of the faithful; the belief that religious relics had magical powers would be challenged; and priests would no longer
be viewed as persons with special divine authority.[3]

Weber saw the reformers as people who would question all
religious practices, and accept none that could not be rationally or scripturally justified. They spurred Christianity
away from the religio-magical and toward the rational-moral.
They changed the emphasis of the worship service from the
miracle of transubstantiation to moral-ethical sermonizing.
They made Christianity more acceptable to the intellectuals of
their day by constructing a doctrinally sound, rationally consistent, and respectably systematic theology.

The Christianity of the reformers made the process of salvation as logical as the laws of jurisprudence. For them, becoming a Christian was based on a clear understanding of the steps in that process:

1. You are a sinner.
2. All sinners must be punished by death according to the laws of God.
3. Jesus died in your place.
4. Consequently, the just demands of God for payment for sin have been met and you are freed from punishment and can enjoy everlasting life.

The penal-substitutionary doctrine of the atonement was all so logical, and it dispensed with all the magical accretions to the Gospel that the reformers claimed had become the essence of Roman Catholicism. For instance, they condemned the purchasing of indulgences as a means of deliverance from sin, as contrary to Scripture and logic. A logically constructed theology was being promoted in place of an irrational magical religion.

What the reformers failed to realize is that their logical approach to Christianity and attacks on the magical traits of the dominant folk religion of their day—a form of Roman Catholicism—gave impetus to the rationalizing tendencies that would come to fruition in the secularism of our modern world. They should have realized that religious faith survives most easily in an environment of magic and superstitions. The world-view of folk religion provides a much better milieu for faith in the transcendental than a world-view that is created through a rational-logical approach to reality.

Perhaps no modern philosopher saw better than did the atheist existentialist Nietzsche that the stern logical theology of Protestant monotheism could destroy the social conditions for religious belief. He perceived that the critical tendency that destroyed belief in all the gods save one created an intellectual atmosphere in which even belief in that one God would soon be called into question.

Calvinism, which Weber considered the purest form of Protestantism because it was the most logical and rational, would
prove to be most destructive of that milieu in which religious
faith was a natural condition. Weber saw that the Calvinists
left little room for miracles in their theology, because they
claimed that miracles belonged to the period prior to the com-
pleting of the New Testament canon.

Furthermore, the Calvinists distrusted human emotions,
and they endeavored to drive emotional expression from their
religious lifestyle. Art, which often gives vent to religious emotions, was suppressed by the dour Calvinists of Geneva, who
claimed that it appealed to the senses rather than the spirit.
Their churches became plain, devoid of sculptures and paint-
ing. No sensual artifacts would be allowed to lure their worshipers away from the things of the spirit. (However, the
suppression of art only served to stifle the religious sentiments
which sought aesthetic channels.)

Herbert Marcuse had the insight that "art depicts what is
absent from the world and makes us discontent with what is
present." He understood that one of the functions of art is to
break the spell of a rational, one-dimensional world and turn
belief in a transcendent spiritual dimension into a desperate
hunger. Art, claims Marcuse, makes us aware of what has been
lost in our world and stimulates a craving for that which is no
more. In a society tending toward secularism, art will keep
alive an appetite for the spiritual. Unfortunately, our Calvinist
forefathers did not see art in this role. Their religion was som-
ber, colorless, and formal; their thinking was exact, logical,
and structured. They were convinced that art would set loose
uncontrollable sensate forces, and this conviction unwittingly
led them to hinder and neglect an instrument that could have
made religious belief easier.[4]

The Implications of the Calvinistic Attitude Toward Work

A contemporary sociologist, Robert Merton, gives still another example of how Protestantism aided the tendency

toward secularism. Merton examines the long-range social consequences of the Calvinistic attitude toward work, and explains how the sanctification of nonecclesiastical vocations increased religious skepticism.[5]

Catholicism had established a distinction between sacred and secular vocations. Those who wished to render ultimate service to God adopted a sacred vocation and entered a monastic order. A sacred vocation required that the individual abandon the normative social and economic activities of the community at large, and live a life separated from the world. The sacred vocations centered in prayer, Bible study, and meditation. To pre-Reformation Christians, there was no higher calling than being a monk or a nun. The majority of the most gifted intellectuals of medieval Europe found their way into monasteries and convents and utilized their talents in these holy activities.

The Protestant Reformation changed all of this forever. The reformed theologians preached that persons could serve God in an ultimate fashion within the context of a secular vocation. These theologians, and particularly the Calvinists, claimed that every man is required to look upon his daily labor as a sacred calling, not just those persons who had been specifically called to serve the church. The Reformers tried to do away with monasteries, only to make the entire world into a monastery. For them, every job, be it farming, carpentry, or the manufacture of clothing, should be rightly regarded as a service to God. And if a person rendered his labor as an act of worship, and believed that God had "called" him to his particular work, then he could consider himself in a sacred vocation.

Merton points out that under the influence of this reformed theology, many brilliant scholars who previously would have gone into monasteries now came to believe that God could be served through a variety of nonecclesiastical academic endeavors. This shift in orientation had particular impact among persons with an interest and capacity for scientific research. Through careful research into the records of the Royal Academy of Science, Merton demonstrates that Puritans were disproportionately represented in the Academy's membership. These Puritans entered into scientific pursuits with a religiously inspired zeal and viewed their discoveries as a means for glorifying God. Furthermore, the theology of the Reformation considered all knowledge to be part of the one system of truth which led to God. This gave still more impetus to the endeavors of Puritan researchers, as they came to believe that their work would shed brighter light on the truths about God. These scientists believed that they were unfolding divine revelations which had hitherto been concealed in nature.

The efforts of these Puritan scientists had unexpected and ironic results. Their religion motivated them to study nature. But the more they studied nature, the more they discovered things that brought their religion into question. In short, Protestant theology stimulated the scientific discoveries which facilitated religious doubt. The concept of an infinite physical universe made belief in a transcendent heaven and a hell problematic. The doctrine of biological evolution raised questions about the necessity for a personal creator. The discovery of germs took away much of the religious mystery and superstitious awe surrounding sickness. These, and many other theories and discoveries that shook the religious world-view of our forefathers, resulted from the work of religiously inspired scientists who viewed their vocations as divine callings. Consequently, Merton argues that Protestantism encouraged the very intellectual developments that helped create a secular world-view.

THE TRAITS OF SECULARITY

The forces and processes that created a secular world-view are manifold, and we have cited only a few of them. However, there is little doubt that the urbane intellectual sector of the Western world has come to accept this world-view, and to live within the context of its basic assumptions. Those of us who would talk about God and communicate our faith to such persons, in a way that allows them to see it as a viable option for a life commitment, must understand the character of secularity.

Langdon Gilkey, in his book *Naming the Whirlwind*, sets forth an inclusive description of secularity by outlining its four essential traits. He claims that the conditions created by these four traits provide an intellectual environment in which modern Christians must theologize and evangelize. These traits are contingency, autonomy, temporality, and relativity.[6]

Contingency

Contingency means that everything that is was caused by some natural phenomenon which preceded it. Those who accept contingency cannot accept the mysterious doctrine of the Judeo-Christian tradition of a universe created *ex nihilo*. According to the premise of contingency, the basic elements of the physical universe must have always existed, and our galaxy, solar system, and planet all developed from them. Out of inorganic matter, amino acids were somehow formed, and from amino acids came organic matter. Through a process of evolution and natural selection, *Homo sapiens* emerged, and man took his place in this universe.

The apparent implication of this account of a contingent creation is that the world and all of its inhabitants were accidents. Supposedly, the process by which they came into being can be discerned through research. The causal chain connecting cosmic dust to the advent of humanity is discoverable by empirical investigation. However, such research can give no satisfactory reason as to why man should have come into being. It attributes no purpose to man, or to anything else that exists. Absurdity rules. The forces and processes that caused all things to come into being may be explained as natural phenomena, but no reason is given for why anything or anyone should exist. This is the legacy of contingency for secular man.

The concept of contingency makes God irrelevant to the creation of the heavens and the earth. It leaves man without the desire to look for religious explanations as to the whence, wherefore, and whither of his existence. Thus, contingency leads to the belief in the second element of secularity—autonomy.

Autonomy

If God is no longer viewed as the essential factor in the creation of the physical universe, the next logical step is the assumption that He is not a factor in the creation of man's social universe. Consequently, secular man believes that he is free to determine his own destiny. There is no divine providence governing his life or the universe in which he lives. His future is his own to mold and there are no goals established by God toward which he should strive. His is an uncharted adventure into the future and the ends and purposes it may have are none other than those which man himself creates for it. Whereas the discarded theologies posted a straight and narrow way for man, and a specific meaning to his life, the autonomous secular man views life as having infinite possible meanings. It is up to man to choose from these possibilities what he will be. He no longer believes in the Calvinistic God who established each man's purpose for being "before the foundation of the world." Autonomy means that man himself defines his ultimate destiny and creates the meaning for his life.

Relativity

An inevitable result of autonomy is relativity. If men are their own creators then the social environment, destiny, and meaning of existence created by one group of people, in one place and time, are not necessarily relevant to another group of people in a different historical context. Those in each society bring into being a system of thought and values that has meaning only for those who create and live within it.

This is particularly true in the realm of morals. The secularists conclude from their crosscultural studies that each society develops a set of behavioral norms which facilitates stable social intercourse for its own members. Normative systems vary from society to society, and there is no single system that can be designated as absolutely binding for all people at all times. Each system of norms is relative to the society in which it applies. There are no longer divinely ordained morals, only socially relative mores. For secular man, the days of absolutes about right and wrong are over. All things are now relative.

Temporality

Finally, secularity is characterized by a sense of temporality as secular man limits reality to what exists in time and space. He assumes an agnostic attitude when he talks about an afterlife or spiritual transcendence. He claims that he can accept only what can be calculated by logic or substantiated by empirical research. He concludes that his life on this planet is all that there is. He concludes that his existence is limited by time. For him there is no afterlife in which the injustices of life in this world will be rectified. There is no future world in which sacrificial virtue will be rewarded. There is no lasting significance to any of his accomplishments. Death is the end of everything, and everything must die. Even the physical universe, like a clock winding down, moves towards maximum entropy in which its present dynamic character will be stilled in an everlasting silence.

THE "FOOLISHNESS" OF THE CHRISTIAN FAITH

There are those Christians who would argue that we should not allow our proclamation of the Gospel to be conditioned by a secular world-view. They claim that there is no need to state our message in forms that make sense to modern man. After all, the Bible itself states that the Gospel is "foolishness to the

Greeks and a stumbling block to the Jews." They assert that
the Holy Spirit makes the message of God acceptable to those
who would be believers. Furthermore, they argue, attempts to
state the Gospel in forms acceptable to those in whom the Holy
Spirit is not active will result in the Gospel being distorted,
even to the point where it is no longer the Gospel. This theological tradition which runs from Tertullian to Karl Barth,
requires simply that the Gospel be stated in faithfulness to the
Scriptures, and that the Spirit of God be allowed to apply its
message to the hearts and minds of those who have ears to hear
it. The first chapter of Romans tells us that those who trust in
the wisdom of this world find it impossible to comprehend the
truth of God.

> For since the creation of the world God's invisible qualities—his
> eternal power and divine nature—have been clearly seen, being
> understood from what has been made, so that men are without
> excuse. For although they knew God, they neither glorified him as
> God nor gave thanks to him, but their thinking became futile and
> their foolish hearts were darkened. Although they claimed to be
> wise, they became fools.
>
> *Romans 1:20–22*, NIV

From the perspective of this approach, apologetics is a vain
intellectual exercise. It is the power of the Holy Spirit, not the
logical reasonableness of the Christian message, that makes
people believers.

There is sufficient validity to this argument to cause me to
ask myself some serious questions. Can a book like this one
really help people to become believers in God? Will my efforts
result in a presentation of the Gospel that distorts God's truth
into heresy?

I do not know if I can answer these questions satisfactorily.
However, I do know that many times young people go off to
college and become confused by what they learn from scholars
unsympathetic to the Christian faith. I find that such young
people often find affirmation for their faith when they under-

stand how faith and knowledge can be integrated. They are spiritually strengthened when they are able to follow the instruction of the Apostle Paul as he teaches, "give a reason for the faith which lies within you."

Another justification for writing this book is to provide some help for persons such as the young woman referred to in the early part of this chapter, who want to believe in God but find it difficult in light of the basic assumptions of their world-view. I believe that the Holy Spirit is already at work in the lives of such persons and while my argument alone will not convince them that God is real, they may remove some of the intellectual barriers to faith. If this book does nothing more than make it easier for some people to come to know Christ, it will have served its purpose.

My intent is to demonstrate that the secular world-view has religious implications in spite of itself. Instead of asking that modern man ignore the traits of the secular mind-set, I ask that he probe them in depth. I am convinced that if he accepts this challenge, he will find more faith than I find in most churchmen.

II

HOW DO CHRISTIANS RESPOND?

3.

Contingency: When the Miraculous Becomes Explainable

Secularism is largely the creation of modern science. The research and theories of those who sought truth in empirical observations rather than trusting ecclesiastical authorities helped to create the widely held assumption that everything could be explained in naturalistic terms. Following the Age of the Enlightenment, many believed that scientific explanations of the origin of man, the development of the universe, and the basis of human behavior would render theological explanations obsolete. This belief that everything that exists has a natural cause that can be scientifically explained is called *contingency*.

In the early part of the twentieth century, Charles Darwin's theory of biological evolution was gaining wide acceptance among educators. Many teachers across the country were beginning to teach evolution to school children. However, this new doctrine would not go unchallenged.

EVOLUTIONISM VERSUS CREATIONISM

Christian fundamentalists believed that this theory contradicted the Bible. Whereas Darwin taught that humans had

evolved over millions of years through a process of natural
selection, fundamentalists believed that God had created
Adam and Eve in a single day. They held to a view now referred
to as "creationism," which suggests that the universe is only a
few thousand years old. These fundamentalists challenged the
right of public school teachers to promote a doctrine of the
origin of mankind which stood opposed to their interpretation
of Scripture.

The resulting controversy was dramatically focused in the
famous Scopes "monkey trial." John T. Scopes, a biology
teacher in Tennessee, decided to test the constitutionality of a
newly passed state law prohibiting the teaching of evolution in
the public school system. He taught his students Darwin's
theory and, consequently, was brought to trial. The ensuing
courtroom battle engaged two of America's most famous law-
yers. On the side of the defense was the brilliant Clarence
Darrow. Championing the cause of the fundamentalists and
supporting the position of the state of Tennessee was "The
Great Commoner" and three-time candidate for the presiden-
cy of the United States, William Jennings Bryan.

The trial became a media event commanding national attention. To the satisfaction of the fundamentalists, Bryan won
the case, but for many, Darrow made fundamentalism seem
ridiculous. He was able to get Bryan to take the stand during
the trial, and it seemed to many that Bryan's literal interpretation of Scripture was ludicrous. Many intellectually sophisticated Christians were embarrassed by the case and repulsed
by the theatrics that accompanied the courtroom procedures.
The case left conservative Christianity appearing academ-
ically naïve.

In the long run, Darwin's theory did not pose as great a
threat to the authority of Scripture as the fundamentalists had
supposed. Many contemporary evangelical Christians have
come to accept the doctrine of evolution while still holding to a
belief in the inerrancy of Scripture. They synthesize the two
explanations of the origin of mankind in a position referred to

as "creative evolution." This theory suggests that God created mankind by means of an evolutionary process, and that the six days in which God created all things actually refers to different epochs in this long developmental process.

Few of those who were engaged in the struggle over evolution comprehended the social and philosophical implications of the theory. They were so caught up in the question of whether evolution proved the Bible fallacious that they failed to perceive that Darwin's thought had some far-reaching ramifications which we are only now beginning to understand.

While Scripture and the doctrine of evolution could be reconciled, the fact remained that Western society had an explanation of the origin of the human race that did not require a belief in God as creator. A belief in a creator could be integrated with the doctrine of evolution, but a belief in God was not essential to the maintenance or consistency of the theory. Darwin's explanation of the origin of the human race could stand on its own. There was now a reasonable and scientific explanation of human origins which did not reach beyond natural causes. Contingency had gained significant credibility.

Social Darwinism

Darwin's thought initiated other changes in the ways we think. Henry Steele Commager, in his book *The American Mind,* gives an excellent survey of how evolutionary thinking changed our thinking about society and gave birth to a new school of sociology called Social Darwinism. Commager showed that, after Darwin, social scientists would no longer view the family, the government, the economic system, the educational system, and other elements of the society as being structured according to some divinely revealed principles. Instead, they would tend to regard each social institution as an evolving entity, constantly improving its structure to become more efficiently suited to the functions that society expected it to serve. The evolutionary progress of social institutions was believed to be dependent on the biological development of the people who made up society. The higher the evolutionary development of the individuals who make up a society, the more highly developed the institutions of that society.[1]

Social Darwinism, on the surface, might appear to be a "value-free" explanation of societal development; however, it eventually provided an intellectual argument for certain forms of racism and ethnic prejudice in the United States. Following World War I, there was a pervasive belief that American culture had a superiority resulting from its white Anglo-Saxon heritage. Many were convinced that the evolutionary process had made the Anglo-Saxon race superior to all others. Furthermore, there was fear that immigrants from southern and western Europe during the early part of the twentieth century would be amalgamated with this superior racial stock and diminish the quality of its gene pool. The resulting race, it was assumed, would establish an inferior culture and the greatness of America would wane.

Madison Grant's book, *The Passing of the Great White Race*, gave what was widely believed to be scientific evidence to support this thesis. One of the most important works of this century, the book helped to generate a hysteria that eventually led the U.S. government to establish immigration laws discriminating against certain ethnic and racial groups, among them the Chinese, the Italians, and the Poles. Many of the leading sociologists of the time, such as E. A. Ross and Albion Small, believed that certain racial and ethnic groups had evolved to superior levels of development. They joined the call for laws that would keep "inferior" types of people out of America. The doctrine of evolution was affecting social policies in ways never dreamed of by Darwin.

Evolutionary Thinking and Contemporary Social Policies

Evolutionary thinking invites questions about contemporary social policies. There are some who argue that the government should not provide welfare programs to assist the socially disinherited. These critics of the welfare state argue that those who have the ability to succeed will do so without government handouts. Inferior persons, they say, should not be encouraged to believe that they are entitled to benefits that their limited talents and substandard character will not allow them to earn. Such critics ask why the better people of society, who have earned what they have, should be heavily taxed in order to provide assistance to people who lack the capacity to help themselves.

These anti-welfare spokespersons claim that the superior individuals can make it on their own, while the inferior ones cannot be helped, no matter how much assistance is provided. They charge that the weaker types consume the resources provided for them by government programs without demonstrating any noticeable improvement in their condition. Government should not interfere with the laws of natural selection. When it does, it only makes matters worse. Social Darwinism gives support to the credo "the government that governs least, governs best."

I remember that as a boy I would often have to listen to my immigrant father rile against welfare recipients. He would tell my sisters and me how he came to America from Italy with nothing but the clothes on his back and twenty dollars. "Nobody did anything for me," he would declare. "I made it on my own! These lazy people on welfare should do the same. God helps all people who help themselves."

The legacy of Social Darwinism influences the approach of some when dealing with the problems of world hunger. I was reminded of this during a visit to a church-related college in Pennsylvania. Some students were then trying to raise money to buy food for starving people in Bangladesh. Their effort was opposed by a prominent member of the faculty who taught economics. Basing his arguments upon the writings of Thomas Malthus (upon whom Darwin drew heavily to develop his theories), this professor claimed that sending food to suffering Third World nations results in more harm than good. He believed that food shipments to a country like Bangladesh only provide the huge population with the sustenance necessary to reproduce and multiply. Instead of millions of hungry people, as there already are today, this economist suggested that there would be even more starving people in the future, as an ironic result of charity programs. There are people, he argued, who do not have the capacity to take the steps to insure their own survival. He said that the whole world would be better off if the population was simply allowed to decrease through natural selection. It was his conviction that the best of these people would survive and, in time, create a viable economy that would allow them to be self-sufficient. He thought that those who could not survive on their own should not be helped to do so. The attitude of this "Christian" professor helped me see clearly that the uses of Darwin's theory by social scientists had moral implications with frightening ramifications.

Elitism

Among those who were fascinated by the moral implications of the doctrine of evolution was one of the founders of modern existentialism, Friedrich Nietzsche. Nietzsche recognized that Darwinian thought suggests that humanity as we now know it eventually will be transcended, and a higher species will one day come to dominate the planet. Just as it was the destiny of the ape to be transcended by man, so it is the destiny of man to be transcended by the superman. Nietzsche predicted that out of the human race there would come individuals whose strengths, abilities, and intellectual capacities would mark them as representatives of a new stage of evolutionary development.[2]

Some of Nietzsche's followers, unfortunately, came to believe that they themselves were members of this higher breed. Suffering from delusions of grandeur, they imagined themselves to be above the "lesser types" of Homo sapiens, disparagingly referred to as "the herd." They viewed themselves as elite individuals, whose ultimate imperative was to realize their highest potentialities, even if this necessitated running roughshod over the mores and folkways of society. As representatives of a new super race, they perceived themselves, in Nietzschean terms, to be "beyond good and evil," as understood by ordinary men and women.

Among those who twisted Nietzsche's thought to serve his own purposes was Adolph Hitler. The leader of the Nazi movement institutionalized Nietzsche as a kind of official philosopher. Hitler used the music of Wagner, which Nietzsche believed expressed the spirit of his thought, as the marching tunes for the Nazi armies. It is said that the soldiers of Hitler's army carried copies of Nietzsche's *Thus Spake Zarathustra* in their knapsacks as they went forward into battle. Undoubtedly, Nietzsche would have been horrified if he had lived to witness the Nazis, who embodied what was diametrically opposed to his idea of the superman, parading as the representatives of a new super race. On the other hand, he should have expected this outcome. If God is dead, as he claimed, then evolution is the law of the universe. In such a universe, the most powerful survive, and the "will to power" is the basic human drive. Evolution suggests natural selection, in Darwin's terms, or "the survival of the fittest," in the words of Herbert Spencer. It is easy to twist such ideas into an ideology that justifies fascist values and to believe that the higher breed of humans are those who are able to conquer and dominate.

In less overtly dangerous ways, the tendency for certain pseudosophisticates to deem themselves an elite, above the rest of mankind, is still with us. A book by Richard Bach, *Jonathan Livingston Seagull*, engendered this arrogance among many of its readers.[3] In the story, a seagull finds that the norms that govern most seagulls keep him from soaring to exhilarating heights, and prevent him from experiencing the thrills of diving at forbidden speeds toward the ground below. Jonathan realized that only by establishing his own rules could he be all that he might be, and experience life to its fullest. Undoubtedly, a host of would-be Jonathans identified with that seagull and believed that they too had the responsibility of achieving that often-misunderstood state of "self-actualization" by ignoring the norms and guidelines of conventional society.

The Negative Implications of Evolution

Sometimes the best way to make a case against a particular theory is to point out what results from following its implications to their logical consequences. This is indeed the situation in dealing with nontheistic versions of the theory of evolution. It is easy to demonstrate that when evolutionary explanations of humanity and society are developed without reference to God, the results are ridiculous at best and horrendous at worst. We have already considered how the theory of evolution without God provided ideological support for the Nazi movement, justifying the "liquidation" of entire ethnic populations on the grounds that they were inferior breeds that should not survive. Humanists, whether they are religious or not, have their sensibilities violated by such practices, and they press for a restating of evolution that does not allow such outrageous results.

In response to this request, we Christians gladly respond by integrating Darwin's doctrine with God talk. We assert that if there is a God who establishes the infinite worth of every person, then there can never be justification for deeming any human being to be a lower form of life which might serve the human race best by simply ceasing to exist. We believe that God loves each man, woman, and child so much that He is willing to die for any and all of them. For us, there can be no super races. We claim that in Christ there is neither Jew nor Greek, neither bond nor free, neither male nor female—all are one in Christ Jesus. While we don't have to prove our convictions in a way that will meet the criteria of empiricists or logical positivists, pragmatically we claim our system works.

We want to convince the whole human race that there is a God who establishes the infinite value of every person, who mystically dwells in every human being and gives to each and every one of us eternal significance. Only then can we develop a reverence for each other that will make an Auschwitz impossible and capital punishment abhorrent. We can't prove that any of this God talk is true, but it represents an option capable of delivering us from the dangerous implications of an elitist evolutionary theory. After all, we never said we have proof. We simply claim that contingency, like the other elements of secularity, leaves much to be desired when constructing an acceptable world-view. We only claim that contingency points beyond itself to something religious.

Believers in the biblical God cannot accept the perversion of Nietzschean thought that leads some egotistical elitists to assume they are better than the rest of the so-called human herd. They know that God is no respecter of persons, and that a despised people like the Israelites are the very ones through whom all nations are blessed. They know that a "pale Galilean," emptied of power, nailed spread-eagle to a Roman cross, is the hope of history. They know that those who would be masters must be servants, that the first shall be last and the last shall be first, and that the ultimate human achievement is to become a "suffering servant" for the sake of others. The value system propagated by Jesus was scorned by Nietzsche and his followers because he thought it was the morality of an inferior race of people. But to those of us who believe in Him, Jesus is the safeguard against an elitism that can easily degenerate into an ideology of oppression.

Christianity leads us to support programs designed to serve the weak and the downtrodden. We become willing to sacrifice to provide for the poor and the oppressed, not out of some noble obligation, but because we sense that God is not only incarnated in Jesus, but also in each needy person who confronts us. We become sensitized by the words of Jesus, which tell us that what we do for unfortunate people, we do for Him

(Matt. 25). For instance, we can never abandon hungry people
in Bangladesh to death, believing that their passing away is
part of the process of natural selection, because we believe that
to turn our backs on such suffering people is to turn our backs
on God. In constructing a consistent world-view for our age we
might have to accept Darwin's way of thinking. But historical
developments in the twentieth century show that a doctrine of
God is the needed imperative to restrain humanity from the
worst implications of evolutionary thinking.

Evolution as Cooperation, not Competition

A whole new approach to the theory of evolution is suggested by some modern sociologists. They critically
investigate the unexamined assumptions which underlie Darwin's theory.

—Why do we understand evolution as necessarily the result
   of competition?
—Why do we assume that there can be no development on
   either the biological or societal levels of existence without a brutal struggle for survival?
—Is there some value system inherent in our Western capitalistic society that predisposes us to assume that pro-
   gressive evolution can occur only if there is laissez-faire
   competition?
—Have certain socioeconomic values conditioned us to accept this theory?
—Is it possible to recast the doctrine of evolution in such a
   way as to make it as scientifically acceptable as the
   Darwinian formula, while making cooperation rather
   than competition the basis of progress?

I first became aware of the extent to which I had ignored
such questions during a conversation I had with some student
leftists at a Latin-American University, where I had been invit-

ed to lecture. Before I could enter the lecture hall, these students confronted me with a battery of questions to determine if I was ideologically fit to speak to their fellow students. Among the questions they asked was whether my biological theories were based on capitalism or communism. That line of questioning was new to me. I thought that biology was an empirical science, free from political considerations. These students pointed out how wrong I was.

In a capitalistic society, they argued, progress results from competition. By struggling against each other, the members of a species go through a process of natural selection whereby the fittest survive. Laissez-faire competition is made to appear as the basis for progress on a fundamental biological level, from a capitalistic perspective. This leads people to assume that laissez-faire competition is a scientifically validated system of progress for all levels of existence, including the societal level.

In a condescending effort to humor these students, I smiled and asked, "And what alternative explanation of evolution do you communists propose?"

"We propose an explanation of evolution based on cooperation," was the answer. "The difference between lower and higher forms of life is measured by the degree of cooperation that has been achieved among cellular units. The amoeba is the lowest form of life because it is the most individualistic. Higher forms of life develop as individual cells give up their separateness and combine to form more complex organisms. The higher the level of cooperation among cells, the higher the form of life."

"What is a human being," one student asked, "but billions of cells harmoniously cooperating?"

He went on to explain, "What is true on the biological level is also true on the societal level. The difference between primitive societies and advanced societies is also measured by the degree of cooperation reached by their members. When individuals turn away from destructive, competitive patterns of life and enter into cooperative relationships, particularly in economic activities, they will achieve a new and higher level of existence. Eventually, nations will learn to cooperate and a new world order will emerge."

I was impressed by this student's argument and his interpretation of evolution. With a quizzical smile I asked, "But who can say which explanation is true? Both are equally reasonable."

"You still don't understand how theories work," he answered. "It's not a matter of which interpretation is 'right' as much as of which best serves the interest of those who hold power. In a capitalistic society, it serves the interests of the ruling bourgeois class to claim that evolutionary progress results from laissez-faire competition. In a socialistic society, we choose to believe that development results from cooperation."

The more I thought about this discussion, the more I wondered if what these students said was true. Why did we in Western societies so readily accept the Darwinian thesis, especially since there were alternative theories available which were hardly given fair consideration? For instance, the French biologist Jean de Lamarck, a contemporary of Darwin, outlined a theory of evolution which did not have the notions of natural selection or survival of the fittest as essential features. His theory, which made cooperation the basis of evolution, was more in accord with the views of the leftist students. Yet Darwin's theory is widely popular, while the Lamarckian thesis has been practically ignored. Could it be that Darwin's theory seemed preferable simply because it legitimated the competitive model of progress of a capitalistic society?

Pierre Teilhard de Chardin

One of the more recent alternatives to the Darwinian system with its requisites of brutal competition is found in the writings of Pierre Teilhard de Chardin.[4] This modern Jesuit anthropologist and theologian believed in evolution, but explained it in such a way that a belief in God was an essential part of the theory. He picked up the much ignored and somewhat disparaged interpretation of evolution set forth by Lamarck. Teilhard, like Lamarck, analyzed evolutionary developments throughout nature and concluded that they could be explained by viewing progress as the result of cooperation. He believed that *Homo sapiens*, for example, is the result of a cooperative arrangement of billions of cells working together in ways that allow for specialization and increased bodily efficiency.

Teilhard knew that a description is not an explanation. He had to know *why* there is a tendency for cells to come together to form higher forms of life. He sought to discover what forces or laws cause this unifying process. As with other parts of his theory, Teilhard found help in his quest in the work of Lamarck.

Darwin argued that evolution takes place on the basis of accidental mutations in certain members of a species. Some of these mutated specimens prove to be more efficiently adapted to their environment, and therefore, have better chances for survival in the struggle of natural selection. In opposition to Darwin, Teilhard restated a thesis of Lamarck, arguing that such mutations are not accidental. He contended that there is something *within* each entity which presses for adaptive change. Teilhard theorized that it is a quality of every living thing to be oriented toward unifying with other members of its species, to form higher organisms with enhanced possibilities for survival.

Lamarck had been laughed out of court by his contemporaries. They believed that his interpretation of evolution necessitated positing some metaphysical presence or force within each living entity in order to explain the drive toward higher and higher levels of development. This criticism did not prevent Teilhard from giving Lamarck's idea fair consideration, and eventually adopting it as an integral part of his system of thought. Teilhard asserted that it was a divine presence and power which determined the tendency toward unification in all living creatures. He believed that God made evolution possible.

Teilhard did not confine his theorizing to the biological level. He observed the same tendency to combine and cooperate in the structure of the atom. He held that electrons are moved to link up with protons to form atoms; that atoms are moved to link up with other atoms to form molecules; that molecules come together to form amino acids; that amino acids produce life; and that eventually human beings evolve. In the development from electrons to human existence, the process of coming together was everywhere evident to Teilhard. He gave this process a name, which became part of a whole new vocabulary he invented for his readers. He called it *hominisation*. The notion of hominisation suggests that love is a force that unites all things. On the atomic level, love is in a rudimentary form and operates without feeling or emotion. As the hominisation resulted in the production of amino acids and eventually in the emergence of life, Teilhard claimed that a new epoch had begun and a qualitatively new and different stage of evolution had been reached. He called this new stage the *biosphere*.

Evolution continues in the biosphere as life "comes together" to create higher forms of life, until a form emerges which is able to achieve self-awareness. Teilhard named this third stage of development the *noosphere*. It is characterized by the development of creatures which are conscious of their existence, and which can even contemplate their own deaths.

Along with Nietzsche, Teilhard noted that it would be unreasonable to assume that evolution culminates in the emergence of human beings. He believed that hominisation continues and that its result will be the unification of humanity as a superior life form. Tapping the biblical vocabulary, Teilhard called this next order of being in the evolutionary process "the body of Christ." To Teilhard, human beings are even now being hominised into a loving, cooperative system, which he believed was well on its way to becoming a reality. He called this emerging stage of evolution the *Christosphere*.

In the Christosphere, humanity realizes its destiny. It is a destiny achieved not in individual self-actualization, but through the creation of a loving community. Human destiny is fulfilled not by the egoistic transcendence of "the herd," as Nietzsche suggests, but by the emergence of a new, harmonized humanity in which people serve one another in mutual submission.

According to Teilhard, Jesus is the model and facilitator of this new humanity. He is what we will all be like in the epoch of the Christosphere. Teilhard claimed that Jesus is an expression of the humanity of the future, which he called "omega man." He believed that Jesus has come out of the future, breaking into our time to reveal the culmination of evolution. Jesus is also the ultimate hominising agent, according to Teilhard, uniting all people in Himself. The presence of Jesus within us leads us to gather together in a new and higher organic grouping, the Body of Christ.

Through Jesus, God is hominising not only man, but all of creation. Everything in heaven and earth is being gathered together into the Christosphere. Salvation is the final result of cosmic evolution, which brings into being a new heaven and a new earth. Teilhard presents us with a view of evolution that delivers us from the dangers of contingency, but still can be integrated with a modern world-view. Teilhard leaves us with many questions, not only about his theory of evolution, but about the orthodoxy of his theology. Nevertheless, he challenges the nontheistic evolutionary theories that have been too easily incorporated into the modern world-view. He brings theology and evolution together in an interdependent system that makes Christ integral to evolutionary development.

THE DEVELOPMENT OF A SCIENTIFIC COSMOLOGY

The tendency toward contingency found support in many of the discoveries of modern astronomers and physicists. The cosmology developed by science helped to create a mind-set that was not particularly receptive to biblical faith. It should be noted that the authors of the New Testament, like other people of their age, accepted and incorporated into their writings a primitive view of the physical universe. They believed that the earth was flat and was encased by a hemisphere called the heavens, which was studded with stars and the Milky Way. Above this hemisphere was the dwelling place for God and the angels, and below the earth was hell, the place reserved for the wicked. However, many contemporary thinkers claim that the theology of the New Testament only makes sense against the backdrop of that ancient cosmology. Bishop John T. Robinson, in his book *Honest to God*, argues that modern scientific knowledge of the structure of the physical universe makes belief in the biblical cosmology impossible. The scriptural doctrines and beliefs which were interwoven with and dependent upon that world view seem no longer tenable to Robinson.

> But now it seems there is no room for him, not merely in the inn, but in the entire universe: for there are no vacant places left. . . . But the idea of a God spiritually or metaphysically "out there" dies very much harder. Indeed, most people would be seriously disturbed by the thought that it should need to die at all. . . . For it is the God of our own upbringing and conversation, the God of our fathers and of our religion, who is under attack. Every one of us lives with some mental picture of a God " out there," a God who "exists" above and beyond the world he made, a God "to" whom we pray and to whom we "go" when we die.[5]

The Collapse of the Ancient View of the Universe

The beginning of the collapse of the ancient view of the universe came with Nicholas Copernicus. Copernicus rejected the belief that the earth was the center of the physical universe. He taught that the earth was a sphere, not flat as was earlier supposed, and that it circled the sun as did the planets and the stars. His heliocentric description of the solar system was revolutionary and soon challenged by churchmen who recognized that it had implications that could prove harmful to religious beliefs.

Martin Luther wrote a tract against Copernicus and claimed that the new astronomy was contrary to the teachings of Scripture. Luther, the leader of the Protestant Reformation, was anxious to replace the authority of the Pope with the infallibility of the Bible. He was convinced that the Bible clearly taught that the sun revolved around the earth, not the earth around the sun as Copernicus suggested. Luther called attention to the biblical story of Joshua's battle with the Amorites. In that story, Joshua was winning the battle as the evening darkness began to fall. Fearing that his enemies would escape in the night, he prayed to God that the sun might stand still and thus allow him daylight time to complete his victory. Luther noted that if the sun did not revolve around the earth, God could not have made it stand still. This argument may seem silly in retrospect, but Luther seriously believed that the authority of the Scripture was at stake in his debate with Copernicus.

The Roman Catholic curia also opposed the new astronomy of Copernicus, but its opposition was more sophisticated. These Catholic leaders argued that by displacing the earth from the center of the physical universe, Copernican doctrine denied human beings, the primary actors on earth, their central place in God's world. The cosmology suggested by Copernicus seemed to leave mankind's importance sharply diminished. The Roman clergy was afraid that the new astronomy signaled a new world-view that would render human beings insignificant creatures in an awesomely vast universe.

Catholic intellectuals recognized that Copernicus's ideas seemed to pose a real challenge to the orthodox religious view of man as the center of God's attentions. Copernicus suggested that human beings inhabit a minor planet, circling an average-sized star that is lost in a galaxy of billions of stars, which is only one of uncountable galaxies scattered through endless stretches of infinite space. The comparative insignificance of human beings in such a universe would make it hard to believe that the entire cosmos was created just to be a setting for human existence.[6]

Threatened by such a challenge, the Roman Catholic Church persecuted any who followed the lead of Copernicus. Galileo Galilei was the most famous of those who experienced the wrath of the Church as it tried to defend itself against science. Utilizing his newly developed telescope, the great Italian astronomer gathered empirical evidence which rendered the Ptolemaic world-view untenable. The Church brought Galileo to Rome and tried him for heresy. However, tradition has it that after he was forced to recant and declare that the earth does not revolve around the sun, he whispered, "But it does move." Critics of Christianity for centuries would refer to the heresy trial of Galileo as evidence that the Church was an oppressive authoritarian institution, willing to suppress any truth that challenged its authority.

The Church scholastics, who were threatened by the new astronomy, may have known more than their modern sophisticated detractors are willing to grant. The world-view of the new science has led many to believe that humans are nothing more than animals which accidentally emerged on a relatively inconspicuous globe, whose only meaning and purpose is what they create for themselves.

Church leaders learned the hard way that the challenges of science cannot be suppressed by heresy trials. History would declare Galileo the real winner of this struggle. Later, Sir Isaac Newton would refine Galileo's views and provide Western society a world-view that defined the universe as infinite and eternal. It was a world-view that survived into the twentieth century. The followers of this Newtonian world-view spoke with such certainty that few could have anticipated that their views would be displaced by new theories and new research. But that is exactly what happened in the first half of the twentieth century. Astronomers and physicists in recent decades have constructed a new world-view that has left the Newtonian cosmology outdated.

Einstein's Expanding Universe

In 1915 Albert Einstein published his work on the general theory of relativity, and prominent scientists set themselves to the task of investigating and comprehending its cosmological consequences. From the ensuing scientific discussions, the belief emerged that the universe is not infinite as Newtonian thought suggested. Einstein's theory required a redescription of the universe as "limited but unbounded." From the time of Newton, it was believed that there are no limits to space and that the stars and galaxies are randomly scattered in all directions. However, the young Einstein seemed totally irreverent towards these cosmological assumptions of Newton and offered a revolutionary new picture. According to Einstein, the universe is to be viewed as spherical and expanding.[7] We can imagine this in terms of a balloon that is being gradually inflated. All the stars, galaxies, and nebulae, and space itself should be considered to be in the expanding skin of the balloon. Such an analogy, however, forces us to ask questions about the larger setting in which this sphere exists and is expanding. Sir Arthur Eddington, of the Royal Astronomical Society, writes with perplexity:

> The super-system of galaxies is dispersing as a puff of smoke disperses. Sometimes I wonder whether there may not be a greater scale of existence of things, in which it *is* no more than a puff of smoke.[8]

If the theory of the expanding universe is correct, we would expect to find that all objects in the universe would be receding from each other. For example, if you were seated in a room that suddenly expanded to twice its original size you would notice that everyone had moved away from you. Your neighbor, who had been seated ten feet away, would now be twenty feet away. In such a general expansion, each person in the room would experience the same thing. Each would observe everyone else moving away from him/her. With an expanding universe, from our galaxy it would appear that all other galaxies were moving away from us. In reality, we would simply be experiencing the results of general expansion.

Surprisingly, astronomers found support for this theory, and their expectations were realized through empirical observations. V. M. Slipher of the Lowell Observatory developed a system to measure the relative movement of galaxies within 500 million light-years of the earth. This method came to be known as the Doppler effect. Slipher found that the recession of the galaxy from the earth could be studied by watching the changes in the color lines observed when the light from that galaxy is passed through a spectrum. Without going into a lengthy, technical explanation of how the Doppler effect works, it can be simply stated that, as a galaxy recedes from us, its movement will show up in a shift toward the red end of the spectrum of its light. Utilizing Slipher's method, and a more accurate method developed by E. P. Ubble of the Mount Wilson Observatory, evidence piled up demonstrating without question that the universe was undergoing just such a general expansion as the followers of Einstein had expected. The theory of the expanding universe seemed to be established on solid ground.

Einstein's theories and related discoveries made it entirely possible to believe that our "limited but unbounded" physical universe is not all that there is. Robinson and Bultmann may have been a bit premature when they concluded that New Testament theology had to be abandoned because it presupposed a cosmology that posited a doctrine of transcendence. Their theologies are more related to the outdated cosmology of Newtonian astrophysics than to the cosmos described in this post-Einsteinian era. It seems ironic to suggest that the mis-

take of Robinson and Bultmann was not that they abandoned
traditional beliefs of Christianity for theology in harmony
with modern science, but that they were not modern enough. If
they had theologized in the context of a more up-to-date cosmology, they might not have dismissed the doctrine of transcendence. The new astronomy has left all of us aware that the
universe can be viewed as existing in a realm that transcends
time and space as we know it.

In the Beginning . . .

There is one other implication of Einsteinian astrophysics
we should briefly explore before moving on in our discussion.
It is important to note the implications of this new cosmology
for the doctrine of creation. If the universe is expanding, it is
likely that there was a time when the process of expansion
started. There must have been a beginning to the universe.
Among those who have theorized about the origin of the universe in these terms was Abbé Lemaitre. This prominent
French astronomer postulated and calculated that the entire
physical universe was once part of a giant photon (particle of
light) which exploded four billion years ago. Lemaitre gives no
hint as to where this giant light particle came from nor does he
have anything to say about what might have existed before it.
Without disputing anything that Lemaitre says, the Christian
might respond to these unanswered questions by recalling the
imagery of the Biblical creation story:

> In the beginning God created the heaven and the earth. And the
> earth was without form, and void; and darkness was upon the face
> of the deep. And the Spirit of God moved upon the face of the waters.
> And God said, Let there be light: and there was light. And God saw
> the light, that it was good: and God divided the light from the
> darkness. And God called the light Day, and the darkness he called
> Night. And the evening and the morning were the first day.
>
> *Genesis 1:1–5*

A SOCIOLOGICALLY BASED COSMOLOGY

While Christian intellectuals struggled to cope with the challenges provided by the natural and physical sciences, an attack on their positions suddenly developed from the social sciences. A survey of academic communities will reveal that religious skepticism will more likely be prominent among those in the sociology and psychology departments than among those who teach biology or astronomy. Starting with I. P. Pavlov and J. B. Watson, a view of human nature has developed that has left little room for the dignity and freedom that are essential characteristics for a Christian theology of man. The most recent debate between religious and intellectual skeptics has resulted from the emergence of a behavioristic model of human existence.[9]

The Christian Debate with the Behaviorists

A Christian view of human nature assumes that people are able to make decisions that determine their own destinies, while behaviorists reject this doctrine. Watson, for example, holds that people are beings which have been conditioned by environment, and thus lack the ability to choose to be other than what they are. In other words, there is no free will. Humans do not *act* according to decisions that they make, but *react* to external stimuli. Where Christianity teaches that we are responsible for our actions, behaviorists claim that we have been conditioned through early childhood training to react to circumstances and situations with specific forms of behavior. Therefore, those who do great things should not be given too much credit and those who commit crimes should not be condemned too severely. After all, the actions of both heroes and criminals are nothing more than programmed, conditioned responses. The saints were trained to behave in a saintly manner; they did not arbitrarily decide to be godly. Sinners sin because they were faultily conditioned and raised to behave in an antisocial fashion. Sinners should not be called on to repent of their evil ways; instead, they should be reconditioned into socially acceptable patterns by a process called "behavior modification."

The most notable contemporary proponent of this behaviorists' view of human personality is B. F. Skinner. His book *Beyond Freedom and Dignity* gives clear and unabashed witness to the behaviorists' view of human nature.[10] He reduces us to mechanistic entities that lack any inner capacity to shape our own actions. According to Skinner, talk about human freedom is poetic, but unfounded. He believes that action is not directed by the will. Instead, we are creatures whose behavior is programmed like that of a robot in Disneyland or that described in some futuristic science-fiction novel. His book is a clear description of what behaviorists think about human beings:

> . . . What is being abolished is autonomous man—the inner man, the homunculus, the possessing demon, the man defended by the literatures of freedom and dignity.
>
> His abolition has long been overdue. Autonomous man is a device used to explain what we cannot explain in any other way. He has been constructed from our ignorance, and as our understanding increases, the very stuff of which he is composed vanishes.
>
> . . . It is often said that in doing so we must treat the man who survives as a mere animal. "Animal" is a pejorative term, but only because "man" has been made spuriously honorific. Krutch has argued that whereas the traditional view supports Hamlet's exclamation, "How like a god!," Pavlov, the behavioral scientist, emphasized, "How like a dog!"[11]

Of course, not all social scientists accept Skinner's point of view or the behaviorists' school of thought. Although there are sufficient grounds to claim that behaviorism is on its way to becoming the dominant school of social thought, many resist its claims and rile against its proponents.

The Social Action Theorists

Among sociologists, social action theorists stand in diametrical opposition to the claims of behaviorism. Max Weber, W. I. Thomas, Rober McIver, and Talcott Parsons are among the major representatives who are committed to social action theory.[12] These social scientists believe that human beings are "deciding" creatures. They believe that we *will* our behavior and are responsible for what we do. They view the task of sociology and psychology as the defining of the social conditions that provide the setting for social action. Social action theorists do not deny that the psychological makeup of the actors and the social circumstances in which they are compelled to act limit the options available to human beings. However, these realities only provide the limits to human behavior. According to the social action theorists, they do not *determine* which of the options actually will be chosen by the actors. Given the makeup of a person in alternatives presented by the social setting, there may be a very limited number of choices available. Nevertheless, there are alternatives, and each person is required to decide from among the options that exist.

It is relatively easy to reconcile the view of human nature held by social action theorists with that advocated by Christians. We too believe that every human being is responsible for his behavior, and that the destiny of every man is determined by the decisions he makes day by day. We too recognize that no one has limitless options (or total freedom), but that each man is able to determine the course of his life by the commitments he makes out of his available alternatives. We believe that ulitmately each man will be judged by what he decides about Jesus.

The Existentialist Response to the Behavioral Theorists

The most passionate opposition to the view of man held by the behaviorists comes not from the social action theorists but from that group of modern philosophers called existentialists. Among the more famous representatives of this group are Martin Heidegger, Søren Kierkegaard, Friedrich Nietzsche, Albert Camus, Martin Buber, and Jean Paul Sartre. Of all of them, Sartre best typifies the kind of response existentialists would make to behavioristic theories of human nature.[13]

Sartre, who coined the term "existentialism," calls the entire behavioristic approach to human nature an exercise in "bad faith." He claims that it leads people to accept their world and their existential condition as though these could not be otherwise. Such an attitude toward human existence results in a resignation to life and a kind of fatalism. It fosters an attitude that leaves people accepting conditions in society and their personal circumstances when they have the ability to change them. Sartre urges each of us to assume responsibility for the condition of society and to commit ourselves to remolding it into a just and humane system. He calls upon every human being to shape his/her destiny through personal commitment. In part, existentialist philosophy is a rebellion against the oversocialized view of man provided by behavioristic psychology.

Despite the fact that Sartre is an atheist, Christians have some affinity for his view. We too believe that persons are responsible for their actions. We acknowledge that there may be social conditions and personal traits that orient people to self-destructive behavior (we call these traits original sin). But we believe that all persons ultimately make choices that determine what they become. This conviction affects our expectations of people and certainly influences the way we counsel people.

A man with marriage problems came to my office. He had been sexually unfaithful to his wife and he had created a horrible mess for himself, his family, and the family of his adulterous partner. As he sat in my office, he showed no signs of repentance. He would not give his wife or me any assurances that he would not be unfaithful in the future. The man explained to me that his parents had never given him the love and affirmation he needed for psychic gratification, and conse-quently, he had an insatiable desire for sexual relations that would sufficiently compensate for this deficiency. Unfortunately, according to him, his wife did not provide enough affirmation and love to meet his needs. He explained he was driven to fulfill his needs in relations with other women. He said he could not help himself. "I do not want to be an adulterer," he said, "but I am driven into this behavior by circumstances beyond my control."

Christians would stand with existentialists and social action theorists and claim that this man cannot so easily escape responsibility for what he is and does. With Sartre they would claim that his behavior is an exercise in "bad faith."

Releasing the Past

George Herbert Mead, an American intellectual seldom given his due, provides some of the most profound criticisms of behaviorism and, indirectly, also attacks psychoanalysis. Mead argues against any system of interpreting human behavior that pays too much attention to the past. While not ignoring the past by any means, he brilliantly demonstrates that what we are is significantly determined by the future. What we envision and hope for impinges on what we are in the present so as to modify our behavior in seemingly unexpected ways. It is this fact above all others that has been downplayed by contemporary psychoanalysts and ignored by behaviorists.[14]

For instance, this summer my son took his place in front of a soccer goal and had a friend continually try to kick a ball past him. He practiced being a goalie by the hour, stopping every shot he possibly could. His behavior should not be understood as the result of social conditioning. He didn't do this because I popped a biscuit in his mouth every time he stopped the ball from going in the net. My son, Bart, is not a Pavlovian dog who simply reacts in ways that have been reinforced by rewards. His behavior could only be explained by the fact that in September he hoped to make his college team and be the varsity goalie. It was what he believed might happen in the future that explained his behavior. His hopes influenced what he did more than his past.

Viktor Emil Frankl was a Jewish psychologist from Vienna who was imprisoned in Auschwitz during World War II. During his years in the concentration camp, he saw that there were many fellow prisoners who gave up the struggle to survive and resigned themselves to death. Others triumphed over the obscene and deplorable conditions of the camp and emerged from their imprisonment to take up life at the end of the war. In trying to analyze the differences between the survivors and those who did not survive, he found that the past experiences of the prisoners did not provide sufficient grounds for establishing the differences. Both groups of prisoners seemed to represent proportionally almost all types of people. Their backgrounds and past experiences were easy to equate. The major difference between those who survived and those who did not was in their respective views of the future. Those who believed that their present sufferings would not end and that the future held only pain and punishment gave up and died. Those who believed that the Nazis would be defeated and that they would be delivered to a better life found the courage to endure. The hope for the future conditioned their ability to deal with the present. It is this understanding of the future and its influence on the present that is neglected by the behaviorists and those in the psychoanalytic school.[15]

Envisioning the Future

Thinkers like Frankl and Sartre are convinced there is an infinite qualitative difference between animals and human beings. Among the traits that separate these creatures is that humans have the ability to imagine what the future might be. Dogs do not visualize their future; therefore they are simply what they are trained to be. Humans can have a vision of what will be and can be significantly influenced by that vision. Animals are controlled by the past, and the past is something that has happened and cannot be changed. Consequently, animals cannot help what they are. On the other hand, humans can project themselves into the future and see alternatives that may be chosen. They know that they can determine their future and experience human freedom.

Envisioning the future is not only the source of human freedom, it is also a source of despair and anxiety. As a human being reflects upon the future, he grows aware that the fear of death has been a source of a host of phobias. Martin Heidegger, the German existentialist, contended that to be human is to live and struggle for meaning in the face of death. He teaches us that, of all the events of the future that influence our present behavior, the greatest is death. The fear of death is responsible for a great deal of our neurotic behavior. For instance, our hyperactivity is one attempt to escape the awareness of our impending end. The accumulation of wealth can be seen as another attempt to shore up security against the ultimate threat of death.[16]

The Christian View

A Christian critique of psychoanalysis and behaviorism has a great deal in common with the doctrines of Mead and the social action theorists. Christians believe that what God promises in the future is a powerful influence on our lives. We believe that what is not yet is more important than what is. We sense the transforming and redemptive results that come from hope.

> Now faith is the substance of things hoped for, the evidence of things not seen.
>
> *Hebrews 11:1*

> For we are saved by hope: but hope that is seen is not hope: for what a man seeth, why doth he yet hope for? But if we hope for that

we see not, then do we with patience wait for it. Likewise the Spirit also helpeth our infirmities: for we know not what we should pray for as we ought: but the Spirit itself maketh intercession for us with groanings which cannot be uttered. And he that searcheth the hearts knoweth what is the mind of the Spirit, because he maketh intercession for the saints according to the will of God. And we know that all things work together for good to them that love God, to them who are the called according to his purpose.

Romans 8:24–28

Christians do not concern themselves as much with where a person is coming from as where he is going. They believe that no matter what a person has been he can become a totally new creature. A transformation can be brought about by that individual's making a commitment to become like Christ. What the individual chooses to become delivers him or her from the scars of the past. This is why Christian evangelists call upon people to give their lives to Jesus. They are calling upon their hearers to will to be like Christ and to commit themselves to doing those things that Jesus would do if He were in their situations.

As a young man in high school, I read a book by Charles Sheldon entitled *In His Steps*.[17] The plot is simple. It describes an ordinary church in which the pastor explains in a Sunday morning sermon that to be a Christian is to do whatever Jesus would do if He were in your shoes. The book goes on to tell of how the members of the church became radical agents of change in their community when they began to live out this challenge.

In many ways I believe that Sheldon's book expresses an important dimension of being converted to Christ. The Christian is someone who decides to follow Jesus. This decision is the beginning of a new life. Of course, there is much more to being converted than simply reorienting oneself to the future. We Christians also have a conviction that the Jesus we seek to imitate is a living spiritual presence who invades our lives and gives us guidance as to what He would do in our circum-

stances. We further believe that when Jesus possesses us, He
gives us inner strength to accomplish our goal of becoming like
Him.

Sigmund Freud and Psychoanalysis

Another approach to understanding human behavior has
been set forth by the psychoanalytical school. Initiated by Sigmund Freud and carried on by a host of followers, it continues
to exercise a strong influence in contemporary social science.[18] Freudians believe that people are molded by the ways
in which they choose to satisfy their sexual desires. Thus, we
are creatures who seek gratification of erotic hungers, and our
behavior must be understood in terms of this libidinal drive.
As infants, during the oral stage of psychosexual development,
satisfaction is sought through nursing. In subsequent stages of
the person's development, the erogenous zones shift to the
anal region and then later to the genital organs. If there is a
normal progression through these developmental stages, the
child will grow into a healthy, well-adjusted adult.

The followers of Freud believe that a troubled adult can
overcome his psychological maladjustments by entering into
depth analysis of his past. Once the individual understands the
events and experiences in his life that have led to problems, he
will be on his way to wholeness. The presupposition of psychoanalysis is that insight into the past causes of a person's troubled state will deliver him from psychological maladies and
render him healthy in the present. Psychologists believe that
this knowledge can save.

Cures for psychological problems, unfortunately, are not as
clear-cut as many Freudians would have us to believe. The
now-famous Hans Eysenck study considered the effectiveness
of the Freudian program for a group of troubled people.
Among those who sought help through psychoanalysis, only 44
percent showed improvement within a year. Among those who

turned to psychotherapy, 64 percent improved within a year. But most embarrassing for the neo-Freudians is the fact that among those who sought no help at all, 72 percent improved within a year.[19] In light of the Eysenck study and a number of others that suggest similar conclusions, we're likely to wonder whether psychoanalysis really offers a cure to emotional and psychological maladjustments or only perpetuates these sicknesses.

Psychoanalysts have become increasingly aware that their system of cure, when effective, works best among articulate, educated members of the upper-middle class. People who have the vocabulary and verbal skills to express their inner feelings and relate their past experiences may find psychoanalysis very helpful in overcoming the negative influences of the past. However, those who lack the verbal ability and sophistication to equip them for the endless hours of talk that go into psychoanalysis can expect little success by this method. The tyranny of the past will continue as long as the individual's crucial experiences remain unexplored and not understood. Thus psychoanalysis appears to provide a way of salvation for dilettantes with plenty of free time for discussion. But the practitioners of this style of treatment can offer little in the way of "good news" for the uneducated working classes.

Responses to Freudian Theory

Freudian systems need not be rejected on pragmatic grounds alone. An empirical criticism of Freud and the psychoanalysts comes from researchers. Anthropologists such as Margaret Mead and Bronislaw Malinowski have shown that many of the psychosexual traits that Freud believed to be universal are actually specifically tied to Western cultures. For instance, the famous Oedipus complex was nowhere to be found when Mead made her famous study of the people of Samoa, or when Malinowski studied the Trobriand Islanders.

Freud's claim to have uncovered the basic nature of all human beings was perhaps too narrowly based on observations of members of European, Victorian bourgeois society.

Research on how well Freudian theories can be applied to people in our contemporary society has proven less than conclusive. William Sewell ran a study to test the effectiveness of neo-Freudian child-rearing theories on families in the Chicago area. Sewell could find no significant differences between children raised in accord with Freudian principles and children who were not. Such findings lead us to ask whether the Freudians are genuinely "scientific," or have simply invented an ideology to support certain child-rearing practices. It should be noted that empirical studies do not *disprove* Freud. But they do suggest that the claim of Freudian theories to provide a *scientific* alternative to Christian beliefs about human nature is both premature and exaggerated. Furthermore, even if Freudian theories gain greater legitimation through scientific research, the results may not be as damaging to the Christian perspective as the Freudians, and even some Christians, might think. There are many who believe that, rather than challenging biblical doctrines, Freudian ideas may, ironically, actually support them. For instance, Freud holds that the original condition of human beings is that of egocentric creatures bent only on their own desire for pleasure. Such a view is much closer to the biblical doctrine of original sin than the romanticized belief in the innate goodness of man that emerged during the Enlightenment. Freudians just might say "Amen" to the description of human nature set forth by the Apostle Paul: "Now the works of the flesh are manifest, which are these; Adultery, fornication, uncleanness, lasciviousness" (Gal. 5:19).

Certainly, Freud sounds more like a Christian theologian than the atheist he claimed to be when he describes human history as being pervaded by the presence of Thanatos (the death principle).[20] He argues that in everyone and in everything there is a tendency towards destruction and death; that everything that exists presses towards the peace that lies in the stillness of death. Freud's insight that death lies within may be understood as a modern expression of what the Apostle Paul states in the Epistle to the Romans:

> For that which I do I allow not: for what I would, that do I not: but what I hate, that do I. If then I do that which I would not, I consent unto the law that it is good. Now then it is no more I that do it, but sin that dwelleth in me. For I know that in me (that is, in my flesh,) dwelleth no good thing: for to will is present with me; but how to perform that which is good I find not. . . . O wretched man that I am! who shall deliver me from the body of this death?
>
> *Romans 7:15–18, 24*

Freud responds to the threat of Thanatos by pleading with Eros (the love principle and the sustainer of life) to rise up against the presence of death. He addresses Eros as though it has personality and will respond to his invocations. In so doing he sounds very much like an Old Testament prophet. Christians believe that love is personal and can respond to our pleas to conquer death. For us this is the essence of the gospel. We believe that God is love and that in His incarnation, crucifixion, and resurrection, Thanatos has been conquered once and for all.

Those in the Freudian tradition have never been quite as deterministic in their view of human behavior as the behaviorists. The Freudians insist that it is possible for each of us to exercise some control over our lives by consciously understanding those past events which formerly enslaved us. While Christians welcome this affirmation of human freedom and mastery, it is not enough for us.

An Alternative Understanding from George Herbert Mead

George Herbert Mead offers an alternative way of understanding the past and its influence on us, allowing for much more freedom than the followers of Freud want to recognize.

Mead teaches that the present condition of a person is not so much determined by the events of his past as it is by the meanings which he gives to those events. While he cannot change the events that have already occurred, he can give those events new meanings, so that thereafter they affect him in a completely different manner.

Mead's point was made clear to me one day as I was walking down a street in Philadelphia. I saw a little boy sitting on the curb, sobbing and wiping tears from his eyes. I sat down next to him to find out what was wrong. He told me that he was sad because his mother didn't love him anymore. When I asked him why he felt that way, he explained that his mother had punished him by giving him a paddling on the rear end because his schoolteacher had reported that he had misbehaved in school and talked back to her in a nasty manner. The boy went on to explain that his teacher deserved to be talked to in a nasty way because she had been so unfair in her treatment of him. He pointed out that even after he explained this to his mother, she still proceeded to paddle his rear end. He was convinced that his mother would not have done that if she really loved him.

I stifled my desire to laugh and took the boy quite seriously. I explained that what he had done to his teacher was wrong, and that loving parents punish their children when they do wrong in order to make them into better people. If his mother had not punished him, it would have been evidence that she didn't care whether he was a good boy or not. But because he had been paddled, he could be sure that his mother loved him and wanted him to be a better boy.

The boy's face lighted up. He was simply overjoyed. He realized that he had given a wrong meaning to the paddling he had received from his mother. She loved him after all. He got up from the curb and happily skipped home to tell her that he loved her too. His emotions were completely changed by his ability to give to the punishment a completely new meaning.

A comparison that I once noted between two adopted children further demonstrates Mead's theory. To one of the children, being adopted meant that he had been rejected by his biological parents. His negative interpretation left him with a sense of worthlessness and a feeling of being unloved. The other child had been told that being adopted meant he was a very special person. He understood that his parents had especially picked him to be their child. This boy had a sense of worth and a feeling of specialness that contributed to his positive self-image and healthy social adjustment. A comparison of these two boys' self-images suggests that for both, being adopted was not in itself the determinative factor. Instead, it was the meaning that was given to the fact of adoption that was of decisive importance. Accordingly, W. I. Thomas claims that what is real in the imagination is real in its consequences. The interpretations we give to the events of the past are more important than what really took place.

By showing us that we can give to past events new meanings and hence alter the ways in which the past events influence us, Mead expands our view of human freedom. He suggests that one can become a new person at any point along life's way. By reinterpreting and reconstructing my past, I can become a completely different person. I am no longer a slave to the past, because I am free to provide new meanings to all that has happened and hence to become completely new. I realize that I cannot change the events of yesterday, last month, or last year, but I can alter the way in which they affect my present condition.

The popular sociologist Peter Berger calls this process of reconstructing the past the "alternation of personality."[21] Christians call it "conversion." With the Apostle Paul, they declare, "If any man be in Christ, he is a new creature: old things are passed away; behold, all things are become new" (2 Cor. 5:17).

To be converted involves a decision to become like Jesus and requires seeing everything in one's past in a whole new light. This may mean that things which were formerly a source of pride are now scorned, and previously insignificant things now take on a new importance. Certainly this was the experience of the Apostle Paul, as he wrote in Philippians 3:7–8:

> But what things were gain to me, those I counted loss for Christ. Yea doubtless, and I count all things but loss for the excellency of the knowledge of Christ Jesus my Lord: for whom I have suffered the loss of all things, and do count them but dung, that I may win Christ.

The human freedom suggested by Mead's description of how we can control the past is the kind of freedom affirmed by Scripture. It is quite easy to understand why a Christian like myself is so attracted to Mead's psychology.

The Continuing Validity of Biblical Theology

Our discussion of contingency was meant to show that modern science has not demonstrated that biblical beliefs have no validity in our modern world. While science may pose some intellectual challenges to biblical theology, I am convinced that the Christian faith is able to meet and survive them all. Scientific explanations of the nature and structure of the universe end up pointing beyond themselves to inklings of transcendence. The doctrine of evolution may end up being nothing more than a description of *how* God created us rather than a contradiction of the doctrine that God is the creator. The social sciences, though still in their infancy, leave us with insufficient grounds seriously to doubt a biblical view of human nature. All in all, the threat of contingency is a manageable challenge. Instead of explaining humanity and the universe as a result of a causal process that makes no reference to God, science just may end up pointing beyond itself to the divine Creator. In the end, science may result in enhancing our state of wonder in the face of the glories manifested in time and space, as expressed by King David:

When I consider thy heavens, the work of thy fingers, the moon and the stars, which thou hast ordained;

What is man, that thou art mindful of him? and the son of man, that thou visitest him?

For thou hast made him a little lower than the angels, and hast crowned him with glory and honour.

Thou madest him to have dominion over the works of thy hands; thou hast put all things under his feet.

Psalms 8:3–6

4.

Autonomy: When Men Become Gods

It can justly be said that the quest for autonomy was the original sin of Adam and Eve. In religious discussion autonomy means being free from the need of God, being the creator of good and evil, and possessing the ability to determine personal destiny. People are autonomous when they appropriate for themselves all the rights and privileges that they previously assigned to God. They are autonomous when they no longer look to a transcendental deity to dictate from a heavenly throne the meaning of human existence, the goals towards which history moves, and the purpose behind tragic and glorious events. Autonomous humanity shapes its own destiny.

THE QUEST FOR IDENTITY

Among modern philosophical thinkers, there are none who embrace autonomy with greater enthusiasm than the existentialists. These advocates of what has become one of the most popular types of modern thinking are so committed to their belief that humans ultimately create the values and the meanings of existence, that many of them find a belief in God intolerable. Atheistic existentialists (and there are other kinds) argue that if there were a God who dictated the values and purposes of human existence, then human beings would lack freedom. If there were a God, they argue, then people would not be at liberty to decide for themselves what is right and wrong, for such things would be divinely ordained. Instead of choosing their own destinies, individuals would be required to submit to the will of the One who designed them. Perhaps the most profound and articulate among contemporary atheistic existentialists is Jean Paul Sartre. A brief summary of some of his ideas will provide us with some understanding of the character of modern existentialist thought and its advocacy of radical autonomy.[1]

The Platonic Inheritance

Sartre argues that modern Western thought is heir to an erroneous philosophical tradition that can be traced all the way back to Plato. That ancient Greek and his philosophical successors gave to Western intellectual history the idea that *essence precedes existence*. In other words, Plato taught that before any of us ever existed here on this earth, the meaning and the purpose of our lives were already established. Each of us had a "pre-existence," in which we were ideal spiritual beings who fully understood who we were and what we were supposed to be. Then, according to Plato, we were born into human flesh, and material existence smothered the essence of our spiritual identities. Under the weight of the flesh, our spiritual identities are buried, and even lost to consciousness. The only hope for salvation lies in the possibility that each of us might be challenged to reflect upon the self and thereby rediscover who he or she really is and is meant to be. The lofty Platonic cry "Know thyself" presupposes that each of us indeed has an eternal preexistent self waiting to be found in the depths of his or her being. In the midst of existence on this planet, one's highest calling is to rediscover the lost and forgotten meaning of life through thoughtful self-analysis and introspection. This Platonic orientation which Sartre strongly condemns seems everywhere evident in the minds of our culture.

I cannot escape the Platonic orientation to reality. I confront it in my counseling with students on a regular basis.

Every May I can count on some student coming into my office, sitting down, looking across the desk at me, and saying, "Doc, I don't think I'll be coming back to school next semester."

Trying to act professional, I'll rip off my glasses and intently ask, "Pray tell—why?"

He'll bury his head in his hands and moan, "I need time, I need time."

If I ask why he needs time, I can predict the answer. He'll say, "I need time . . . time to find myself." Sometimes it seems as though most of the young people in the Western world are trying to find themselves.

The student almost inevitably goes on to say, "Doc, I'm tired of playing all the roles that have been prescribed for me by society. I'm tired of being the person my family expects me to be, the person the church expects me to be, the person the school expects me to be, the person my friends expect me to be. I've got to peel away each of these socially prescribed identities. I've got to peel away each of these socially imposed selves. I've got to peel away each of these socially dictated roles. Then maybe I can come to grips with the core of my personality, the real ground of my being."

When confronted with such a passionate tirade, I usually respond with a retort provided by Paul Tournier and say, "Fella, suppose that after you peel away each of these socially prescribed identities, after you tear away each of these socially imposed selves, after you peel away each of these socially dictated roles—you discover you're an onion!"

Now that's a real possibility. For just as an onion is nothing more than the sum total of its skins, so it may be that the human personality is nothing more than the sum total of all the roles that person has learned to play. It just may be that after you strip away all of your socially prescribed identities and take the long journey into your inner self and get there—hi ho, nobody's home! After you play the introspective games prescribed by the campus guru and explore to the innermost recesses of your personhood, you just may find an abyss of nothingness.

If there was such a thing as a self waiting to be found, undoubtedly by now someone would have come along and found it. You would expect that out of the hundreds of thousands of young people who take time off to find themselves, one of them would come back and say, "Hey, Doc, I did it. I looked and looked and finally found myself!"

But the reason this doesn't happen is that no such thing as a self is waiting to be found. Rather than waiting to be discovered, the self is waiting to be *created*. And there is only one way to create a self, an identity, a meaning to one's life, and that is through commitment. Show me somebody with a clear-cut commitment and I'll show you somebody who knows who he is and what life is all about. I have yet to meet a person who has dedicated his life to Jesus Christ without reservation who lacks an identity or a purpose for being. I have yet to meet a person who has said, "For me to live is Christ, to die is gain!" who doesn't have a definite image of who he is. The problem is that most people would rather play the game of self-discovery than make a genuine commitment, for commitment costs everything a person is and has.

The Question of Ultimate Meaning

While an atheistic existentialist such as Sartre would not accept my belief in God, he would certainly agree that the ultimate task in human existence is to create identity and meaning through commitment to that which the individual believes to have ultimate significance. Sartre might even approve of the narrowness of my commitment as I claim that

Jesus Christ is the *only* way, the *only* truth, and the *only* life. For, argues Sartre, a commitment will never provide meaning and personhood for the individual, unless the individual is convinced that the object of his commitment is the ultimate truth, not only for himself, but for all people everywhere and in all times. Only a commitment to what is believed to be universally true can provide the individual with the confident assurance that he knows what his life is all about. There is a fanatical quality about the genuinely committed person, for he believes that he has dedicated himself to the only valid way of life.

I agree with Sartre's method of establishing meaning. I differ from him in my belief in God, but concur with his conviction that the meaning of one's life is not established a priori to existence.

I suggest that the God who is revealed to me in the Scriptures, rather than dictating my raison d'être, invites me into a dialogical relationship with him out of which the meaning of my life will be created. I believe that Jesus makes me His brother and entreats me to share my dreams and aspirations with Him while He reveals His hopes for me. For me, prayer is a dialogue in which I interact with God, and with Him evaluate the various choices and options which confront me. In this mystical relationship, I gradually become aware of the pros and cons of each alternative, and even have new options opened to my consciousness. I believe that God tells me that the decision is ultimately mine. Willing me to be free, He allows me to choose an option that might displease Him, while giving me the assurance that even when I fail, His grace affirms me and invites me to choose again.

"Finding God's Will"

Let me describe for you what usually happens at the youth meetings and retreats at which I speak. Almost always, someone takes me aside in a private discussion and asks, "How can I discover the will of God for my life?" Such a question assumes that what a person is supposed to be and do has been already established for him by God. The seeker thinks that his only problem is that he doesn't know how to find this preexistent purpose and meaning. He is convinced that if he could only figure out how to discover God's preordained meaning for his life, he could escape life's ambiguities. My response is that the Bible does not promise the kind of personal revelation that he is seeking. I argue that the Scripture teaches that living by faith is like being willing to work out, in fellowship with Christ, a plan of action for *today*. To be a follower of Jesus Christ is to *not* have a grand plan for the rest of one's life, but to be totally committed to walking with Jesus, daily seeking His will, hourly working out one's salvation with fear and trembling. It is to be open to the possibilities inherent in each existential moment and to believe that commitment to Christ can be expressed today in ways that were totally undreamed of yesterday.

Most of the Christians I know readily testify to the fact that just a few years ago they did not have the slightest idea that they would be doing what they are currently doing. Furthermore, they point out that they are glad they didn't know, for otherwise they might have been overwhelmed with crippling doubts about their abilities to meet their new challenges.

I believe that to be a Christian is to live with a kind of freedom that Sartre himself would have to admire. It is to wake up in the morning and ask God, "Well—what shall we do today?" The Christian does not view life as the acting out of a play that was written a long time ago. Instead, God invites us to collaborate with Him in writing the script, and to lean on Him as the perfect prompter when the time has come to act. Sartre's call to abandon a belief in an essence that precedes existence does not pose as much a threat to my Christian lifestyle as a first reading of his work might suggest.

To summarize my position, I believe that God calls us to make the choices that determine our lives. Unlike Sartre, however, I do not believe that these choices must be made alone. To live by faith is to make life's decisions in the context of a fellowship with One who loves me and gave Himself for me. The Christian is free from the tyranny of a predetermined identity and purpose, although he is not autonomous in the full sense, for he is committed to a relationship in which God and he, as friends working together, create the meaning for his life.

Rather than undercutting the foundations of Christian belief, Sartre's vision of autonomy actually helps us to understand the complex nature of Christian freedom. To all of those Christians who are waiting for God to reveal what He wants them to do, I say choose a course of action from the multiplicity of options that are available to you at the present hour, and as you choose, be sensitive to God's reactions to your choice.

IMAGES OF GOD

The secular belief in autonomy has still deeper implications for human existence. The modern secularist not only believes that we have no access to a preexisting meaning to our lives but also questions the very existence of a God who can relate to a person endeavoring to create meaning for his life. This tendency toward agnosticism is encouraged by many scientists and intellectuals who urge that God is nothing more than the result of wishful thinking or neurotic delusion. While leaders in many academic disciplines support religious skepticism, in the last half-century the most serious challenges to a faith in the existence of God have come from social scientists. Freud in psychology and Emile Durkheim in sociology describe religion by naturalistic explanations with which all intellectual Christians must deal.[2]

Freud's Picture of God

Freud proposed that God is nothing more than the imaginary projection of the father figure. The child looks to his father to supply his needs, to protect him from danger, and to answer all of his questions. When the child has reached adulthood, he still longs for the comfort and security of an authoritative father figure. Consequently, in his neurotic imagination, he creates a god to fulfill his psychological needs and desires.

The link between the human father and God appears more baroque and fantastic when the sexual implications of Freud's theory are spelled out in his portrayal of the Oedipus complex. While this explanation may seem a bit far-fetched to many, I think it is important to review Freud's ideas in order to provide the Christian with a basic understanding of one of the most commonly promoted explanations for the origin of God in the academic community.

Freud writes that before the dawn of history human beings lived in hordes. The male who was the strongest ruled the horde, and all others were forced to comply with his wishes. Power was the only basis of the social organization. The dominant male appropriated all the female members of the group as his mates, and he enjoyed exclusive control of their sexual favors. This sexual monopoly led to such jealousy and anger on the part of the other males, the "sons" of the horde, that eventually they rebelled, banding together to kill and eat the male authority figure. By this murderous deed, the sons had hoped to rid themselves of the tyranny of the father. But they were not so easily freed; they now suffered from guilt. The memory of their father haunted them and they became more frightened of him dead than they had ever been when he was alive. To appease what they believed to be the anger of their dead father, they made some pledges, and these pledges mark the beginning of religion and civilization. The guilty sons agreed to venerate the dead father's memory and to reimpose stringent sexual restrictions upon themselves, in a nostalgic conformance with the original system of authority. They promised to worship the father's spirit and to mate only with women who had not been his sexual partners, with women outside their group. These pledges form the basis of the two elemental taboos of totemic cultures: the taboo against killing the totemic animal and the taboo against incest.

Freud believed that what was true in the history of the human race is repeated in the psychological life of every individual. He believed that every son sexually desires his mother, the mate of his father. The child views the father as all-powerful, and realizes that he cannot compete with his father for his mother's sexual attention. He attempts to escape this frustrating predicament by identifying with his father and idealizing him in his imagination. This idealized image of his father becomes his image of God. But rather than successfully resolving the conflict of desire and guilt, this idealization, this father worship, actually serves to perpetuate the psychological dilemma of the child. And this perpetuation of psychic ambivalence is the basis for all of religion, according to Freud.

God the Father

Those of us who are involved in Christian education are very much aware of the fact that there is a correlation between a child's concept of God and his perception of his father. If his father is authoritarian, the understanding of God will reflect that reality. On the other hand, if the father is loving and full of grace, the child's conception of God will reflect those characteristics. The Freudian's point that a God concept is tied up with a father concept is well validated by observing the beliefs about God of boys and girls in any Sunday school class.

My own response to the challenge of Freud's theory of the origin of religion is to point out that it does not so much explain away the existence of God as describe the process by which our understanding of God is molded by the circumstances of our early childhood development. Freud does not prove that there is no God. He only explains why we view Him as we do. Freud is helpful in enabling us to understand what we must deal with when we introduce children to the God described in Scripture and revealed in Jesus Christ. Consequently, I view Freud's contribution as a help rather than a hindrance to the task of proclaiming the Gospel.

The arguments of Freud never really seemed convincing to me. While his basic premise that an individual's image of God is based on his image of his father did make sense, I found it very difficult to accept his theory of the religious implications of the Oedipus complex. Furthermore, a reading of Freud's work makes it quite clear that he was not as free from religion as he pretended to be. The values of his Judaic heritage are evident in most of his works, and he gives many hints of a repressed belief in transcendental powers, belying his declared stance as an enemy of religion.

The Durkheimian Thesis

Having come to terms with Freud's challenge to my faith, I thought I had handled the best argument against the existence of God that social science had to offer. But it was the work of Emile Durkheim, one of the founders of modern sociology, which proved for me the more serious challenge.

In its most simplistic form, the Durkheimian thesis of religion is that God is nothing more than a symbolic representation of the collective energy and dominant values of the society that worships Him. Any image of God, according to Durkheim, is characterized by those traits which the society of worshipers value most among themselves. Consequently, religion is nothing more than a process whereby a group ends up worshiping itself.

Durkheim's views are best set forth in his book *The Elementary Forms of the Religious Life*. In this sociological classic, Durkheim analyzes the social development of a tribe of aborigines. He notes that the members of this primitive society considered certain human traits to be desirable to possess. They wanted their children to have these traits, and they did their best to encourage the development of the desirable characteristics throughout the socialization process. Durkheim observes that the group came to associate the traits they collectively valued with a particular animal, which he calls a "totem." He notes that in totemic cultures, the totem animal soon comes to be worshiped as a god. However, if the deity of the tribe is nothing but an animal that symbolically incarnates the collective values of the social group, it follows that in worshiping such a god, the tribe is really worshiping itself.

Furthermore, the tendency towards totemism is not restricted to primitive societies, but is evident in cultures throughout the world. Even in our own society we tend to ascribe human qualities and social traits to animals. It seems a natural thing for us to talk about being as wise as an owl, as sly as a fox, or as subtle as a serpent. Whereas the Bible teaches that man is created in the image of God, Durkheim suggests that God is created in the image of society.

In my personal observation of American religion, I find strong validation of Durkheim's thesis. I visit hundreds of churches of various denominations each year, and, as I listen to preachers describing God, I often get the feeling that the Jesus they present is more of an incarnation of the dominant values of the American society than an incarnation of Yahweh. Jesus tends to be transformed by American preaching into a white, Anglo-Saxon, Protestant Republican who promotes laissez-faire democratic capitalism.

It is interesting to note that the WASP mainstream of American culture is not alone in its totemistic tendencies. American minority groups show the same inclinations. For several years I taught Sunday School in a black Baptist church, and a picture of Jesus hung on the wall of my classroom. I think the picture came from Billy Graham's *Decision* magazine. It depicted the Lord looking very much like Charlton Heston with a beard. He had a faraway look in His eyes and seemed to embody the characteristics of American rugged individualism. This Jesus was a WASP, without the slightest sign of Semitic ethnic characteristics. One Sunday I entered the classroom and discovered that the familiar picture of Jesus was gone. In its place, someone had tacked up a new picture in which Jesus was portrayed as a black man.

"Who put that there?" I demanded.

"I did," responded one of my black students. He wore sunglasses, his neck was ringed with several strings of African beads, and he had an afro that seemed to take up half of the room.

"Jesus wasn't a black man," I said.

"Well, he wasn't no honky either," the student pointed out. I realized that just as I wanted Jesus to represent my social heritage, this young man wanted Him to represent his group.

I know of a Chinese Catholic church that has magnificent stained glass windows. However, as I studied the image of Christ in the window over the main altar, I noticed something that struck me as very strange. This Jesus had Chinese eyes! He was an Oriental man, dressed up in the robes of ancient Israel. I chuckled at the idea, but had to ask myself some serious questions. Is it any more absurd to make God into a Chinese man than it is to make Him into an American? For that matter, why do I even think God is a He? Doesn't the masculinization of God say something about the dominant values of my society?

No Graven Images

Durkheim's discoveries about religion provide us with a new understanding of the biblical admonitions against making graven images of God. For it is impossible for any image of God that arises in human consciousness to express the nature of the divine without bearing the marks of the values and perspectives of the culture which produces it. The theologian Paul Tillich even warns against the idolatry of verbal descriptions of God found in theological writings, for they too tend to be essentially descriptions of the dominant traits of the culture. However, the totemistic tendencies observed by Durk

heim were noted almost two millennia ago by the Apostle
Paul, who wrote in his Epistle to the Romans:

> Because that, when they knew God, they glorified him not as God,
> neither were thankful; but became vain in their imaginations, and
> their foolish heart was darkened. Professing themselves to be wise,
> they became fools, and changed the glory of the incorruptible God
> into an image made like to corruptible man, and to birds, and four-
> footed beasts, and creeping things.
>
> Wherefore God also gave them up to uncleanness through the
> lusts of their own hearts, to dishonor their own bodies between
> themselves: who changed the truth of God into a lie, and worshiped
> and served the creature more than the Creator, who is blessed for-
> ever. Amen.
>
> *Romans 1:21–25*

For many, Durkheim's theory proves to be a devastating
attack on religion. Durkheim seems to demonstrate conclusively that religion has no transcendental origin, but is totally a societal creation. If that be true, then, it follows that
God is merely a projection of the collective consciousness of
the group, that worship is nothing more than collective effer-
vescence, and that religious conversion is simply an emotional
surrender to a different cultural perspective. However, is it not
a better argument that Durkheim's writings do not so much
negate the possibility of believing in a transcendent, eternal
God as explain the origin of the false deities against which
Christianity must struggle? Durkheim helps us to see that in
each social system there emerges a cultural deity which com-
petes with the biblical Yahweh for the allegiance and devotion
of the people. In truth, the idol created by cultural religion
poses a more serious and subtle threat to biblical Christianity
than secular agnosticism. For agnostics are not deluded into
thinking that they are believers, but cultural religion leads
people to think that they are indeed Christians worshiping
Yahweh, when in reality they worship a symbolic representation of themselves.

In my own personal theology, I believe that the idol of cultural religion is the *Antichrist*. He is the one who leads many astray, seducing them into the dominant values of the society while keeping them from the awareness that there is a living God who is the enemy of what they worship. While I taught at the University of Pennsylvania, I tried to share the gospel with many of the faculty members and students. Very often, the response to my witnessing would be a claim by the individual that he once believed in God, but his growing sophistication led him to reject such an idea. I would always ask such a sophisticated atheist to describe for me the God that he had rejected. When he had finished doing so, I would congratulate him and tell him that I too reject that God. I would go on to explain that the God he had rejected is not the God described in Scripture and revealed in Jesus Christ, and that now that he was rid of his false god, he was in a better position to encounter the real one.

I would inform him that, in many ways, the God he would find in Scripture would contradict all of his previous notions of what God is like, and would challenge him to a lifestyle diametrically opposed to that prescribed by our dominant culture. Whereas in America the cultural deity offers prosperity to his followers, the biblical God calls upon us to sacrifice all that we have for the poor and suffering peoples of the world. Whereas the American cultural deity invites self-aggrandizement and self-assertion, the biblical Lord calls us to be meek and humble. Whereas our cultural deity allows us to be comfortable in our society and to affirm its values, the God of Scripture requires that we sacrifice all that we are and have in the cause of transforming the world into a kingdom in which the hungry are fed, the naked are clothed, the sick are cured, and the needs of everyone are met.

It is important to note that since the cultural deity legitimates the existing social order, those who oppose our values are therefore enemies of this God. When we go to war, we can be sure this God is with us—after all, He is one of us. He stands for the American way because we made Him in the image of

America. But the biblical God stands opposed to this cultural
deity, and presents an alternative value system, outlined in the
Sermon on the Mount. The God of Scripture renders us enemies of the religion instituted by our society, so that when our
nation goes to war, Christians have the audacity to declare
that our Lord is not an American and that He loves our enemies as much as He loves us. Furthermore, we claim that the
biblical God calls us, too, to love our enemies, and to do good to
those who would hurt us. In short, I argue that the God rejected by many atheists is the God that Durkheim described so
well, the God created by our culture. On the other hand, the
God of Scripture, whom these atheists have failed to consider
properly, is radically different.

Depending on the a priori assumptions of his readers, Durkheim's theories seem to point to different conclusions. Those
who seek to be rid of God, in order to enjoy the kind of radical
autonomy advocated by Sartre, find justification for their
stance in Durkheim's analysis of religion. However, Christians
can use Durkheim as a means of understanding the origin of
the false gods that emerge *sui generis* in our society, and so
better enable us to fight this idolatry. The Durkheimian de-
mythologizing of cultural deities helps us to differentiate between the transcultural eternal Lord and the socially created
alternative, which must be rejected by Christians.

BRAVE NEW WORLD

In his effort to establish the kind of radical autonomy which
he believes to be a prerequisite to freedom, the modern secularist believes that he must be free from the belief in the existence of a transcendental deity. To that end, he gravitates
toward theories that enable him to dispose of God as a psychological or societal manifestation. The thinkers who have given
birth to modern existentialism encourage this move to autonomy, being convinced that it is an essential step towards the

development of a new and more responsible humanity. Atheistic existentialists believe that only when we realize that the oppressive social system in which we live is of our own making, and not ordained by God, will we be prepared to assume the responsibility of changing that system. Only when we realize that there is no God dictating personal destinies will we be free to address ourselves to the Herculean task of creating meaning for our lives. Only when we realize that there are no established absolutes will we create the kind of norms and values that will enhance the humanity of everyone.

The challenges that the existentialists define for the autonomous secular individual are indeed inspiring and thrilling. They seem to call for a new "religious" lifestyle. Autonomy seems to invite the individual heroically to create a "brave new world" in which each person's humanity will become self-actualized. It means adopting a new creed, but one which is intended to be free from the kind of magical and mystical qualities that smack of divinity, and seem to have no place in this modern world.

The Anxieties of Autonomy

But there is another, darker side to autonomy, and the very thinkers who celebrate its liberating potential also provide the most eloquent descriptions of its terrible threats and dangers. One of the most famous of the founders of modern existentialism, Søren Kierkegaard, contends that the anxieties created by autonomy are so overwhelming that they can drive a man to make a fanatical leap into religious faith as the only viable option.[3]

Kierkegaard's keen observations of the modern world led him to conclude that, for most of the human race, the freedom that accompanies autonomy would prove to be more of a curse than a blessing. Kierkegaard saw that as man came to realize that his destiny is determined by his own choices, he would be filled with anxiety. Faced with the necessity of choosing the

meaning of his life, without the assurance that he was choosing rightly, the individual would be filled with fear.
Kierkegaard knew that the numerous options available for
personal commitment could so paralyze the individual as to
render him incapable of making any decision at all.
Kierkegaard called this dreadful predicament, resulting from
autonomy, *angst*.

In prophetic speculations on life in the twentieth century,
Kierkegaard predicted that most people would desperately
seek to escape from the freedom that was so psychologically
traumatizing. As he peered into the future, he saw that modern
man would become hyperactive, engaging in a multitude of
senseless forms of entertainment in order to be distracted from
the burden of freedom. People would try to evade the truth
that they had not yet decided on the meaning of their lives,
even though time was slipping away from them and death was
moving ever closer. Kierkegaard realized that individuals
would gladly conform to the lifestyle, values, and meanings
prescribed by the social system, rather than face the loneliness
and terrible responsibility of having to choose ultimate meanings for themselves. For most people, autonomy would create
the conditions of a psychological hell.

Escape from Angst

Kierkegaard believed that in the quest to escape angst and
find a fulfilling meaning to life, every person must go through
three stages. The first of these he called the aesthetic stage,
wherein the individual seeks fulfillment in passionate experiences. Art provides the values and terms by which the aesthetic individual seeks to achieve a kind of humanizing ecstasy
that would make life worthwhile. Craving "peak experiences,"
the aesthete involves himself in music, literature, and paint-
ings. Passionate involvement with the work of a great com-
poser seems to transport him from his psychologically
debilitated state into the fullness of being. The aesthete tries to
savor from his existential experiences gratifications that will

give ultimate meaning to his life. He moves hungrily from experience to experience, from person to person, constantly seeking something new.

But Kierkegaard knew that the individual could not find real authenticity and fulfillment in the aesthetic stage. There would come a time when not even Mozart would gratify him. Having exhausted the potentialities for ecstasy inherent in the passionate living of life, he would become bored with all that aesthetic experiences can offer. His boredom would produce a yawn that would eventually turn to a scream. The individual would become aware that there must be more to life than aesthetic sensations. Not every aesthete would manage to reach this crucial point. But any who did would be ready to move to the next stage in the quest for being, which Kierkegaard called the ethical stage.

In the ethical stage, the individual seeks fulfillment through good works and acts of charity. He commits himself to creating the Kingdom of God on earth. He strives to alleviate hunger, to bring hope to the suffering world, and to do the work of Christ in every situation. Trying his best to gain a sense of aliveness in service for others, the ethical individual seeks to establish his identity by fulfilling his moral duty. But in the end, his attempts at good works fail, and he is left with a sense of emptiness and with a feeling of futility. This is because he realizes the perverseness of his own nature as he fails to live up to his ethical aspirations. He recognizes that no matter how hard he tries, his sinful character makes the ethical life an impossibility for him. Only when he comes to this crucial awareness can the suffering pilgrim be ready to make the leap of faith into the third stage, the religious stage.

The "Leap of Faith"

For Kierkegaard, being religious means much more than believing the right doctrines and endeavoring to do things which the church advocates. Rather, the religious individual is one who becomes radically committed to God, in what

Kierkegaard calls a "leap of faith." This commitment is intensely personal and may lead him into a lifestyle at odds with the expectations of those who live within the context of institutionalized religion. Without any assurance that it is indeed God who dictates his action, without any objective proof that he is being obedient to the leading of the divine, the religious man follows what he believes to be the leading of the Spirit. Each moment, he is filled with the fear that he might be doing the very opposite of what God wills. The emotional and intellectual condition of the religious individual is one of radical insecurity. But Kierkegaard does not seek an escape from this subjective suffering that goes with being religious. Instead, he embraces it, believing that this is the essence of the religious condition and the basis of full humanness.

To illustrate what Kierkegaard meant by the leap of faith, I have often told my students the story of Blondin, the great French tightrope walker who lived in the latter part of the nineteenth century. Blondin once strung a tightrope across the Niagara Falls and before ten thousand screaming people inched his way from the Canadian side to the United States side above the roaring, cascading Niagara River. When he stepped on U.S. soil, ten thousand people chanted his name, "Blondin, Blondin, Blondin."

Blondin raised his hand and quieted the crowd. Then he said, "I am going back across the Niagara Falls on the tightrope, but this time I will carry someone on my shoulders. Do you believe in me?"

The crowd called back, "We believe! We believe!"

Blondin once again silenced them and asked, "Which of you will be that person?"

Everyone fell silent. Then, out of the crowd, came one man. He climbed onto Blondin's shoulders and allowed the tightrope walker to carry him back across the rope to the Canadian side of the Falls.

Ten thousand people had cried, "We believe, we believe, we believe." But in the end, only one really believed. Belief is more than just intellectual assent to propositional statements about reality. Believing is dangerously and radically giving yourself over to that in which you believe, without any evidence to assure that you have decided rightly.

Kierkegaard himself provides a parable to illustrate this faith commitment that makes a person truly religious. He describes his boyhood experience of being taught to swim by his father. Splashing wildly with both arms, kicking with one leg, he called to his father, "Look at me, look at me. I'm swimming!" But, says Kierkegaard, all the time he was holding onto the bottom of the swimming pool with his big toe. It was Kierkegaard's conviction that most of those who call themselves religious are not religious at all. Many of us pretend to be people of faith while failing to abandon ourselves completely to God. We may practice a culturally approved morality, and even believe the "right" things, but this is not enough. To be truly religious, Kierkegaard claims, we must hold onto nothing, and surrender ourselves totally to the promptings of God's Spirit. Such a leap of faith must be the religious struggle of each and every individual, for God's will can only be known subjectively, and followed in aloneness.

I believe that Kierkegaard made an invaluable contribution to our understanding of the ramifications of the autonomy encouraged by modern secularity. Kierkegaard saw that autonomous man was not as free from God as he might appear to be. He realized that, because of the sinful nature of people, all of man's efforts to achieve self-fulfillment are doomed to failure without God. The radical freedom promoted by autonomy thrusts man into an existential condition of angst from which he can be delivered only by a radical leap of faith. Instead of destroying religion, autonomy actually enhances the conditions which drive people into the arms of God.

The Importance of Christian Community

My understanding of the New Testament leads me to believe that Kierkegaard made one serious mistake in his handling of existential problems. That mistake was his insistent emphasis on the privacy and loneliness of the religious individual. I would like to submit that Kierkegaard failed to understand what the Bible says about Christian community. He did not adequately recognize that Jesus does not ask us to make life's decisions in isolation, but calls us to follow Him in community. The community ordained for this purpose is the Church. As outlined by Scripture, the Church is a gathering of radically committed believers who realize that any subjective prompting of the Spirit must be confirmed by a group of fellow believers before the individual dares follow its leading. The Bible teaches us to "test the spirits to see if they be of God." Elsewhere, the Scriptures teach that the way to test spiritual promptings is to share them with other Christians, with confidence that if all are agreed that the leading is of God, it is proper to obey the call.

Although his emphasis on personal decision and responsibility is invaluable, Kierkegaard failed to develop a biblically sound theology of the Church. For though the Christian may be suspended above 100,000 fathoms of nothingness, he does not face his existential predicament by himself. The Lord does not require the Christian individual to guess about His inscrutable will without help or support. On the contrary, though the Spirit speaks privately, in a soft, still voice, the Christian can find validation for his inner promptings in the affirmation of a community of believers. The Church can provide the assurance that what the individual believes to be the will of God really is the will of God. For the Bible tells us that "wherever two or three are gathered together in His name, He is there in the midst of them."

From my own experience, I can testify that a small body of believers can help to assure that the spiritual promptings which lead me to make important decisions about life are really of the Lord. I have three close friends, and at least once a week we get together for breakfast. At these breakfast meetings, we share with one another the circumstances, problems, and situations in our lives that require decisions and action.

Each of us, in turn, shares what he thinks God wants him to do, in light of the existential situation in which he finds himself. After careful thought and intensive reflection, the other members of the group share their feelings about the proposed course of action. When we are all agreed that what the individual is planning to do is in accord with the will of God, he has some assurance that he is doing the right thing. He is still following the inner leading of the Spirit, but he does not do so in a state of aloneness. He is supported in his action by this body of believers which the Bible calls the Church.

There have been countless times that my small group of Christian friends has provided affirmation and support for personal decisions I have had to make, and has given me a peace and confidence that Kierkegaard would find difficult to understand, and perhaps would even condemn as an evasion of existential responsibility.

Unfortunately, most Christians do not submit themselves to the authority of a body of believers in the process of making life's decisions. For instance, most of the clergymen I know reached their own conclusions that God wanted them in church vocations. Very seldom do I meet an individual who is a minister of the gospel because a group of believers helped him to discern his gifts and honestly confirmed the fact that God had called him to be the pastor of a church. The Book of Acts shows that New Testament apostles and preachers did not individually decide that they had been called to these tasks, but heeded the communal decisions of the Church which confirmed their calling.

It is no wonder that the contemporary Church has many clergymen who ought never to have been ordained. In all probability, if any of these misplaced servants of God had been part of a fellowship in which there was a loving willingness to be honest, they would have found little confirmation for their personal inclination toward a clerical vocation. Having tested their intended plan in the context of Christian fellowship, such persons might have found that God's will for their lives lay in another direction.

The Christian Option for Hope

Modern man, with his secular consciousness, seeks personal authenticity in autonomy. Yet autonomy proves to be a curse as much as a cause for celebration. While holding out the promise of radical freedom, it promotes an existential condition of unbearable doubt and anxiety. Faced with the freedom to choose for himself, autonomous man suffers agonies of hesitation and second-guessing. He craves an authoritative voice to tell him who and what he should be. He longs for the kind of confirmation that can best be found, according to the New Testament, in the community of the Church. While existentialists point out the psychological misery to which autonomy leads, the Christian faith which so many of them repudiate offers a viable option for hope. I believe that the more that modern man investigates the nature of existential autonomy, the more he will come to recognize his need for the leading of the Holy Spirit, confirmed by the Body of Christ. For where Sartre declares that there is "no exit," Jesus tells us, "I am the way, the truth, and the life; no man cometh unto the Father, but by me."

5.

Temporality: When Nothingness Becomes a Terrible Something

For the secular man everything is temporal. All things pass away. Every creature dies. There is no everlasting life, and nothing is eternal. Life is a purely natural phenomenon and when the biological process has run its course, death is the natural conclusion. There is no heaven; there is no hell; there is no afterlife. In the end, there is nothing at all. It may be hard to face up to this reality, and down through the ages men have sought ways to evade it. Religion, according to the secular thinker, is sometimes deliberately invented in order to offer the hope of an afterlife to those who lack the courage to face up to their own finitude. To the secularist, belief in an afterlife is nothing more than wishful thinking. He tries to be brave as he makes these assertions, but beneath the surface, he suffers from profound fears and anxieties.

THE AWARENESS OF DEATH

Young people characteristically try to evade the threat of death and nothingness by refusing to face the fact that they too will one day die. Avoidance of their own deaths seems to make it easier to talk about death. I am often amused at the apparent ease with which my religiously cynical students can say that this life is all there is. It is hard for the young collegian to comprehend his own mortality and grasp the significance of his own finitude. To him, dying is what happens to older people. It doesn't happen to him and his friends. Logically, he knows that one day he will die, but he lives so detached from that fact that it barely affects him. He lives as though time will be forever and there will always be a tomorrow. Looking at the clock and watching its hands go around and around without stopping, it is easy for him to delude himself into thinking that for him there is no end to time. Perhaps it was better when people checked the time by looking at hourglasses, for then they were always reminded that time runs out.

One afternoon several years ago, I met with a class of students in a course on existentialism. We were discussing death and the threat that it poses to living a meaningful life. In turn, each student shared the effects that the knowledge of his death had upon the way in which he lived. In this class, largely made up of young students, there was one middle-aged woman. She waited until last to speak and then began by telling the others that they really didn't know what they were talking about.

She said, "One time I went to an organ concert where one of the organ notes got stuck. At first, I hardly noticed it. It was only during the pauses in the music that one could faintly hear its sound. But as the concert progressed, the sound of the stuck note got louder and louder until it was no longer possible to enjoy the music. That one note ruined everything.

"That's the way the reality of death has affected me. When I was younger, I only thought about it at those times when I had nothing else to think about. In the melancholy pauses of my existence I would reflect on the fact that someday I might die. But as the years passed, the awareness of my death became more and more pronounced. I came to be aware of it not only during the pauses of my life, but even in the midst of the routine activities and enjoyments of life. Eventually the awareness of death became so powerful that it has permeated everything I do and think, and rendered me incapable of enjoying anything."

The class fell silent. They knew that the woman was right—they did not truly know the power or meaning of death. As secularists they believed that there is nothing on the other side of the grave. They blithely accepted the dictum that everyone moves toward annihilation. But now they had been made to realize that they were too immature to understand what the fact of death eventually does to us all.

The secularist claims that at the other end of life there is nothing, but he sometimes fails to see that one cannot face this prospect with neutrality. The nothingness which he posits after death seems to rush towards him and passes judgment on everything that he has done or tried to be. He knows that his lofty dreams, his greatest achievements, and his meaningful experiences all will come to nothing. This is a judgment that is difficult to accept. As time passes and death approaches he senses a futility to everything. Helmut Thielicke once said that New Year's Eve proves to be increasingly difficult because it reminds the mature man that his life is slipping away. Thielicke says, "On New Year's Eve men must make noise in order to drown out the macabre sound of grass growing over their graves."

Søren Kierkegaard compared life to a smooth flat stone thrown over the surface of a pond. The stone dances and skims over the surface of the water until that moment comes when, like life itself, it runs out of momentum and sinks into nothingness.

Escape Attempts

I had always objectively believed, like any reasonable person, in my own mortality, but one night when I was thirty-one years old, it hit me in a special way. As I laid my head on my pillow to sleep, I was overwhelmed with a horrible realization.

"Tony," I said to myself, "you're one day closer." I felt a trem-
or run up my spine. I hated the thought and did my best to
suppress it. And it is just to escape this thought that so many
people endeavor to preoccupy themselves in a hyperactive lifestyle. They constantly seek forms of entertainment aimed at
distracting them from the unbearable truth of their own mortality. But the effects of the threat of death continue to haunt
them, if not consciously, then subconsciously, producing a
host of displaced phobias.

Blaise Pascal, the fifteenth-century mathematical genius
and mystic, once said, "All evil stems from this: men do not
know how to handle solitude." Pascal recognized that in solitude it is especially difficult to evade the sting of death. Consequently, men avoid being alone as though the escape from
solitude were the most urgent task to be undertaken.[1]

The funeral industry, particularly in America, is able to exploit the craving we all have to evade the confrontation with
our own impending nonbeing. We want the funeral director to
do everything he can to communicate the impression that the
loved one is not dead, but only sleeping. We want the corpse
dressed up in the best clothes and surrounded by flowers and
sweet-sounding music. Sometimes we carry off this charade so
effectively that it takes months for the deluded friends and
relatives to face up to the fact that the deceased is really dead
and will not come walking in the door in just a little while.

On college and university campuses across the country,
there are courses on death and dying. Taking the lead from
Elizabeth Kübler-Ross, they make an attempt to study death
objectively.[2] Kübler-Ross suggests that dying can be reduced
to specifically defined stages, a theory that gives the illusion
that outsiders can understand what the dying person is going
through. I guess such courses have their place, but I agree with
Kierkegaard's declaration that "no man can die my death for
me." No sociological study can help us to die by making gener-
alizations from a mass of data collected from dying inter-
viewees. For death is the most subjective of experiences, and

nobody, save one, has ever returned to tell us about it. The existentialists are right in their insistence that dying is something each person must face alone, in his own distinctive way.

The impact that our temporality has upon our everyday lives is a subject of growing interest. The popularity of Gail Sheehy's book *Passages* reflects this concern.[3] In this bestseller, Sheehy points out that men and women often experience what she calls a mid-life crisis. As they come to a growing awareness that their lives are slipping away from them and death is not far away, they become desperate to deliver themselves from the effects of passing time. Sheehy demonstrates that the increasingly common marital infidelity among men in their early forties is often an attempt to recover lost youth and to gain new possibilities through an exhilarating romantic fling. If these men can prove that they are capable of seducing younger women, they can temporarily assure themselves that they are not getting old after all.

Sheehy also analyzes the effects of temporality on women as they approach middle age. In our sexist society, women are often left feeling that the loss of youthful beauty diminishes their worth as human beings. Consequently, as they find their bodies aging and they lose the ability to turn men's heads while walking down the street, many women fall into deep depressions.

Sheehy explores these depressions and gives graphic descriptions of the pain and agony that middle-aged women experience as they become sensitive to the ways in which aging is affecting them. These aging women want to believe that they are indispensable to their husbands and children. But deep down inside, they know that one day death will overtake them. The time comes for each woman to be put into a black hearse, driven out to a cemetery, dropped in a hole, and have dirt thrown in her face. And after it is over, the crowd of mourners will return to the church and eat potato salad and chicken in the fellowship hall. Middle-aged women sense this fate approaching and become increasingly sad. They try to fight off the aging process with torturous diets and intensive exercise. They try to conceal the effects of passing years by covering their faces with pancake makeup and coloring their cheeks with rouge. But these efforts are doomed to fail eventually, and depression sets in as these women feel that they are becoming increasingly obsolete.

Everyone in our society must face the growing awareness of temporality that debilitates the modern secular individual. The bravado that characterized his earlier declaration of independence from religious beliefs becomes increasingly hollow as he senses death overtaking him. He may attempt to put up a good front and declare his ability to live courageously in the face of death and eventual nothingness. Yet one senses tremors in his voice, an unarticulated fear that eats away at his emotional well-being like a cancer.

Accepting the Inevitable

One existentialist, Martin Heidegger, endeavors to see some positive consequences arising from the nihilistic view of temporal existence that typifies the secular mind-set. Heidegger argues that Christianity cheapens life in this world by suggesting that it is only a prelude to a richer and better eternal life after death. If this is true, then earthly existence need not be really taken seriously. Heidegger condemns this belief because it keeps people from realizing the ultimate significance of every moment of every day. The Christian doctrine of eternal life diminishes the need for people passionately to live this life to the fullest. According to Heidegger, it leaves people unappreciative of life.[4]

Such unappreciative people are like the members of Emily's family in Thornton Wilder's *Our Town*.[5] Emily, the main character of the play, discovers too late the singular joy of just being alive. After her death, Emily is allowed to watch herself relive one day of her life. She is warned that she will not enjoy what she experiences. Nevertheless, she embraces the opportunity and chooses to relive her twelfth birthday. However, seeing the way her family members take each other for granted and live with so little passion is so painful for her that she finally pleads to be delivered from it all. Looking back on her family and her life one last time, Emily cries out, "Good-bye, good-bye, world. Good-bye, Grover's Corners . . . Mama and Papa. Good-bye two clocks ticking . . . and Mama's sunflowers; and food and coffee; and even ironed dresses and hot baths . . . and sleeping and waking up. Oh earth, you're too wonderful for anybody to realize you." She stops, hesitates, and then, with tears in her eyes, asks the audience, "Do any human beings realize life while they live it?—every minute?"

Heidegger believes that until a person comes to grips with his own death and realizes its consequences, he is not capable of realizing life in a way that does it justice. It is only in the face of death that he becomes fully alive, because it is only in the face of death that he addresses himself to life with the glorious intensity that makes him fully human.

I must admit that what Heidegger says about the effects of the Christian doctrine of the afterlife makes a great deal of sense to me. So much is this the case that I have changed my theology about what happens when I die, so that my view of the afterlife can contribute to the meaning of my life here and now. Perhaps I can best explain my view of the Christian doctrine of eternal life by another illustration from my teaching experience.

The Christian Doctrine of Eternal Life

One day in class, I asked my students a simple question: "How long have you lived?" The students had no idea what I was driving at and seemed irritated that I would waste their time with such a trivial question. Nevertheless they answered me. One of them said he had lived twenty-two years; another, twenty-one; and so on.

"No, no!" I responded. "I didn't ask you how long you have

existed. I asked you how long you have *lived.* There is a big difference between living and existing. You may have existed for twenty-two years, but you have lived very few moments. Most of your life has been a meaningless passage of time between isolated instances when you were fully alive.

"When I was twelve years old, my school class was taken to New York City. Among the things we did there was to take a ride to the top of the Empire State Building. Thirty-five of us raced around the walkway at the top of the huge edifice. We played racing tag. We shouted and screamed at each other and we all were having a great deal of fun. Then, for some reason that I don't understand, I suddenly stopped. I walked over to the rail of the walkway and grasped it tightly, and stared at the awesome expanse of Manhattan below me. I concentrated on the scene with great intensity. I focused all my energies on creating a memory of what I was experiencing. I wanted to fix it in my mind forever. I lived that moment. I experienced the scene that lay before me with a heightened awareness. I know that if I could live for a million years, that experience would still be a part of me. That moment was lifted out of time and eternalized. Unfortunately, I have lived too few moments with that kind of full awareness.

"I'm sure you know what it's like to want to capture a moment in time and eternalize it. Perhaps you were with your lover. The ecstasy of lovemaking made the moment so precious that you wanted to hold onto it forever. It was one of those 'I-Thou' encounters so eloquently described by Martin Buber.[6] A moment in which the separation between you and your lover was overcome and you sensed a oneness as fulfilling as any experience described by religious gurus. You know what I mean when I talk about eternalized moments. You have lived some of them and have longed to live many more. Now let me ask you my question again. How long have you lived?"

There was silence in the class and then one student said, "Maybe a minute, maybe less. I guess I haven't lived much at all."

My belief about the afterlife is that when I die, I will carry to the other side of the grave all of the moments that I have eternalized during my natural existence. This means that every moment of every day has ultimate significance, for each moment has the potentiality of being eternalized. Every human experience has the possibility of being lifted out of time and made part of everlasting life. I find it a moral imperative to take life seriously, to live it intensely, to taste it passionately, and to enjoy it fully. To do otherwise would be to allow my life to be nothing more than "hay, wood, and stubble," which will be consumed and reduced to nothing when my time on earth is over. However, if I live with the kind of passion that Heidegger suggests, if I live with total awareness and "redeem the time," then at death all of this will remain with me.

> For other foundation can no man lay than that is laid, which is Jesus Christ. Now if any man build upon this foundation gold, silver, precious stones, wood, hay, stubble; every man's work shall be made manifest; for the day shall declare it, because it shall be revealed by fire; and the fire shall try every man's work of what sort it is. If any man's work abide which he hath built thereupon, he shall receive a reward. If any man's work shall be burned, he shall suffer loss; but he himself shall be saved; yet so as by fire.
>
> *1 Corinthians 3:11–15*

Jesus Christ the Deliverer

I have found that there are two conditions that prevent me from experiencing life as my theology dictates. The first is guilt and the second is anxiety. Guilt keeps me oriented to the past. It focuses my attention on the things that I should have done, and the things that I should not have done. Guilt is a burden that saps my energy, dissipates my enthusiasm for life, and destroys my appetite for savoring the fullness of each moment. Anxiety, on the other hand, orients me to the future and keeps me from enjoying life in the present, because of the dread that I have about the future. Caught between guilt over the past and anxiety over the future, I have nothing left with which to address the present moment in which I find myself.

When I meet people, they are sometimes left with the feeling that I am absent, that I am "not really there." Despite my physical presence, I am really somewhere else in time and space. That's why I need Jesus.

The Gospel is the good news that Jesus delivers me from my guilt, and the past no longer need torture me. I am not simply referring to the biblical fact that Jesus died on the cross for my sins, and so I need not fear that my sinful past will catch up with me. More important, the Jesus declared in Scripture is one whom I mystically encounter, who invades my person-hood, and who provides an inner deliverance. My sin is forgiven and forgotten, buried in the deepest sea and remembered no more. Any who read the testimonies of Christian converts will discover, over and over again, references to the wonderful freedom from guilt that accompanies their new life in Christ.

But there is further good news declared in the proclamation of the Gospel. Jesus not only delivers me from the effects of yesterday's sin, he also delivers me from the anxiety that makes me reluctant to face the future. The old cliché suddenly becomes meaningful as I recognize that "I do not know what the future holds, but I know who holds the future." I live with the biblical promise: I commit my life to Jesus, my ultimate future.

To be saved is to have a relationship with Jesus through which I am freed from guilt and anxiety, so that I can live each moment of each day with the exciting aliveness that the Scripture promises to the sons and daughters of God. This is what it means to be "born again." I am freed to eternalize moments of my natural existence that they might become everlasting life.

NEW WAYS OF TALKING ABOUT TIME

I know that the secularist will find very little in my response to the challenge of Heidegger to allay the anxieties that accompany his comprehension of the ramifications of temporality. Having excluded metaphysical doctrines from his discussions of human existence, the secularist realizes that he has no basis for believing in eternal life. Marxists try to tell him that his personal significance after death can be established by helping to create a proletarian utopia to be enjoyed by future generations. But he longs for far more. Anthropologists try to show him that his desire for eternal life is derived from a heightened sense of individuality, peculiar to Western cultures, which does not exist in all societies. But this explanation only tells him *why* he craves eternal life and does not deliver him from his resentment of death.

There are, however, some new ways of talking about time that can help the secularist to cope with the threats of temporality. Surprisingly, recent research and developments in some of the academic disciplines he most respects point to the possibility of eternal life. In some branches of psychology there seem to be intimations of immortality. In the field of astrophysics, one of the corollaries of Einstein's theory of relativity suggests that eternity might be a dimension of time, and another holds implications that provide some supports for a theology of the afterlife. If the secularist is willing to explore the implications of these disciplines, he may find deliverance from the gloominess that usually accompanies serious modern discussions of temporality.

Phenomenology and "the Self"

There is growing interest in a school of psychology called phenomenology. This trend is largely due to the rediscovery of the works of George Herbert Mead, whose analysis of human consciousness is pregnant with implications for our discussion. Mead, whose work we began to explore when dealing with contingency, calls upon us to examine "the self" in an objective fashion, giving careful consideration to the process whereby each of us comes to self-awareness.[7]

According to Mead, the human personality should be considered as having three components. The first of these is the body—that corporate entity made up of billions of nerves and sinews, a host of functionally related organs, and a complex sensory system.

The Body as "Thing"

I can observe my body as a thing, or an object, in the world. When I do this, it becomes like any other thing and can be structurally examined, physically dissected, and chemically analyzed. As an object for empirical study the body holds the attention of biologists who have made a science out of studying its makeup and function. I seldom look at my body objectively (thank God); however, there are rare occasions when my subjective involvement with my body is temporarily suspended. On those occasions I am aware of the "thingness" of my body, and from a somewhat detached posture I sense with strange fascination the objective character of my corporate being.

One such time was when I smashed the thumb of my left hand in the process of closing my car door. My thumb was so mangled that I had to go to the hospital. There they administered an injection that so thoroughly numbed my arm that all feeling from my shoulder down was completely lost. The doctor took a piece of cloth, cut a hole in it, and shoved my thumb through the hole. I could see it there, two feet away from my eyes, yet in no way could I see or feel that it was attached to my body. The doctor proceeded to sew up my wounded thumb and do his best to restore it to health. As I looked at it out there, two feet away, I had to keep telling myself, "That thumb is *me*. It's part of my body. They're sewing *me* together." In that particular situation, I became aware of just how "thinglike" my body really is. It became blatantly clear that my body was an object in the world.

Sometimes when I am sleeping I roll over on my arm in a

way that cuts off the blood circulation. When this happens, my arm "goes to sleep," and when I wake up there is no feeling in it. My arm seems to hang from my body without being a part of it. My brain can still send my arm instructions so that I can lift it and flex it, but I cannot feel it moving or flexing. When I touch my face with it, it is as if I were being touched by another person. I can feel my face being touched; I cannot feel my hand touching it. It is as though I am not subjectively involved with my hand. I give it orders as though it belonged to someone else, and it obeys like a willing slave. But I do not feel it as a part of me. I view it as an objective thing.

Some of the meditation techniques prescribed by Zen Buddhism and other forms of Eastern religious thought also can enable an individual to "transcend" his body. Without one's necessarily getting mystical or spiritual, these techniques can enable an individual to relate to his body as an object to be studied or a corporate entity which can be observed in a detached fashion. This thing, called the body, is part of what comprises "me."

The "Stream of Consciousness"

The second component of my personhood that Mead would have me consider is my stream of consciousness. This is the "thing" that I describe to the psychoanalyst when he asks me to lie on his couch and tell him whatever comes to my mind. My stream of consciousness is a succession of events, ideas, and experiences that I call into my memory out of my past. This flow of images and ideas of all that I have encountered or thought is also part of "me." It too has a "thinglike" quality to it and can be analyzed objectively. I can tell you all about "me." I can describe the various aspects of "me" to you. I can tell you what goes through my mind, what hurts "me," and what brings "me" enjoyment. While you do not have direct access to "me," I do. I can talk about "me" to you in much the

same way as I just talked about my body. While this component of "me" is not subject to empirical analysis, I still view it
as an object.

As I look at "me" as an object in the world, I immediately
become aware of the fact that there is a difference between the
"me" that is being viewed as an object and the subjective "I"
that observes "me." I realize that this may sound like a lot of
double talk, and indeed it is complex. Nevertheless, I urge you
to stay with me in this discussion, because I believe that it has
fruitful possibilities.

The Interaction between "I" and "Me"

Mead wants us to understand that the self is a process of
interaction that occurs between the subjective "I" and the
objective "me." "Me" is the repository of all the objective data
of my existence. Every idea that I ever thought, every feeling
that I ever felt, and every event that I ever encountered are
gathered together to establish "me" as an exciting creature in
the world. Nevertheless, I am aware that "I" am other than
"me." I can look at "me" and observe "me" in a quizzical
fashion. "I" can see what changes have taken place in "me,"
yet I know that "I" am the same.

I meet a friend from my childhood days who asks, "Tony, is
it really you?"

"It sure is," I respond. "Everything about 'me' may have
changed, but 'I' remain the same."

Every organic particle of my corporeal nature is different
from that which was known to my friend. He is looking at an
entity totally different from the one he viewed thirty-five years
ago. My thinking has changed. I don't believe the same things.
I am a Christian now. "Everything has passed away and everything has become new" in my consciousness, yet I tell my
friend that "I" am Tony Campolo. While everything about
"me" has been altered, transformed, and reconstructed, I
know that "I" am the same Tony Campolo who was once
friends with the man who now views me as a stranger.

The differentiation that exists between "me" and "I" is easily ignored by students of human personality. This is probably one reason why many psychoanalysts fail in their attempts to understand and help people. When one psychoanalyst asks me to tell him all about myself, I might enthusiastically cooperate. I may go to great lengths in my efforts to tell him about "me." I might tell him about all the events of my yesterday, relating to him things that are both ordinary and traumatic. I might tell him who loved "me" and who did not, what I thought and what I had been taught, what I felt and what I failed to feel.

But I know that after I explain myself to him in detail, after I tell him all that there is to tell about "me," after I have dredged up from my past all those things that have molded me into the Tony Campolo of the present, he still does not know who "I" am. I know that he knows all about "me," but "I" have evaded him. The "I" that has described "me" to him remains alienated, estranged, and apart. For "I" cannot be known as an object. "I" am not a thing. "I" refuse to be there in the world for someone to analyze. "I" can only be known by encounter and subjective involvement. Every once in awhile, "I" enter into a relationship with another person and become aware of the fact that "*I*" am known to that person and that person is known to me. While everything about "me" changes, there is ultimate quality about who "I" am, for "I" remain the same— constant amid the passing of time.[8]

By the use of the imagination I can separate the "I" from the "me." For instance, I often ask myself, "I wonder what it would be like to be you for a day." What I mean by that is much more than living life in your body. I mean what it would be like to think your thoughts, to reflect upon your stream of consciousness, to experience your feelings. I wonder what it would be like not to be me, but to be you instead. Furthermore, I sometimes ask myself why I was born me and not you. Why was I born to possess this stream of consciousness and this body? What would it be like to be born someone else? There may even come a time in my existence when I reject me or find myself unbearable—in which case I might try to adopt the identity of another. Perhaps in a psychotic state I might choose to be Napoleon or Caesar rather than being me. Such are the games that "I" can play with "me," for "I" am free to be anything "I" choose, while what is true about "me" is as fixed as are all events that belong to the past.

There is a difference between relationships in which people know "me" and those in which they know who "I" am. Recall the ways in which you have related to people and the ways in which people have related to you. Consider the fact that there have been people who have known a great deal about you. They are acquainted with your personal history. They have watched you grow and develop. They have kept track of your education. They know your relatives and friends. And yet you know that even though they know all about you, such persons may not really know you at all. Contrariwise, you may have a chance encounter with a person, perhaps on a bus, in an airplane, or in a cafe. You talk, you share and express a few of your convictions and afterwards you sense that this has been no ordinary discussion, no ordinary exchange. There was something sublime about it, something mystical, ecstatic. You know that you have been known and that you knew the other person in a way that transcends objective data. Of such encounters, the Apostle Paul writes: "Now we see through a glass, darkly; but then face to face: now I know in part; but then shall I know even as also I am known" (1 Cor. 13:12).

Lao-tzu, the ancient Chinese philosopher, described a conversation he once had with a man in which he asked whether or not the man loved his wife. The man answered, "Of course I do." Lao-tzu then asked the man to describe his wife. The man complied with the philosopher's wish, telling in detail about her physical traits, describing how she thought and explaining her character and personality. When he had finished, Lao-tzu said, "You do not love her, for if you loved her, you could *not* have described her."

At first the response of Lao-tzu might seem strange, but on

further consideration its profundity becomes clear. The objective things about a person that can be related and discussed are superficial and have little to do with the essence of who the person really is. When you love someone, you know that the person is so much more than the sum total of all the objective characteristics that comprise that person's personality. Ultimate intimacy with that person occurs when the "I" that transcends "me" establishes a oneness with the "I" of the other person. Martin Buber, one of the most important of the religious existentialist thinkers, has written extensively on such a relationship.[9] He refers to the "I" of the other person as "Thou." His famous book *I and Thou* is a classical attempt to express the nature of such an encounter.

The "Now"

If you have been able to follow our discussion to this point, you are able to distinguish between the "I" and the "me," and you are now ready to deal with the ways in which it is possible to discern some of the transtemporal qualities of the "I." First of all, "I" do not exist in the past or in the future. "I" exist *now*, and now is not a part of time. I cannot say that the next minute is now or the next second is now, or even the next millionth of a second is now. Now is the nonexistent point that separates the past from the future. It has no extension in time. It is not a segment of the temporal. Nevertheless I know that now exists, because it is where "I" am. No wonder Augustine once wrote: "There is nothing that I know better than now. It is more real to me than any other time and yet when I reflect upon it, it doesn't exist at all."[10]

Immanuel Kant, likewise, was overwhelmed by the perplexities surrounding the problems of time with specific reference to the character of the now. In his *Critique of Pure Reason*, he sees that nothing is more real and existential than the now in which I live, and yet he senses that now is not a segment of the flow of history.[11]

Nothing that "I" experience can be known objectively. I cannot even tell you what "I" am thinking now if you should ask, for I must reflect upon what "I" am thinking now, and in that process of reflection, my thoughts become part of my past. I can only tell you what "I" *was* thinking when you asked me, "What are you thinking now?" I sense that while everything about "me" evolves, changes, decays, and passes away, "I" remain an unchanged essence with a seemingly indestructible character.

There is no way of proving that "I" will continue to exist after you have put the remains of "me" in the grave. But when I consider this possibility, I gain intimations of immortality. Furthermore, I sense that because "I" live in the now, that "I" will always be, because now always is. Now never was, nor will it ever be. Now is not part of the temporal, yet it seems "I" am eternally there.

A skeptic might respond to this line of reasoning by arguing that even if this discussion made sense, it wouldn't solve the problem. He would likely contend that his fear and trembling about death is caused by his belief that now will cease to exist for him. He says, "Without 'me,' 'I' cannot exist. And when you bury 'me,' 'I' will be no more, and will not be alive now or ever again."

In order to address this complaint, our discussion must shift from the insights of phenomenological psychology to those provided by recent developments in the field of astrophysics. Once again we look for help in the work of Albert Einstein, and specifically in his theory of relativity.

Einstein's Theory of Relativity

Up until the development of Einsteinian physics it was assumed that in all places and in all situations and circumstances, time would be experienced in exactly the same manner. If there were creatures with consciousness throughout the universe, it was believed that they all would be experiencing the same inexorable flow of time. We thought that whether a conscious creature was on earth or on some planet in a solar system located in a galaxy billions of light-years away, the passage of a day would be experienced in the same way. However, such common-sense thinking was challenged and refuted when Einstein proposed and gave evidence for his new theory.[12]

The new physics of Einstein challenges us to understand that time is relative to motion. The faster I travel relative to you, the more slowly time will pass relative to you. Let's put it this way: If I were to get into a rocket ship and travel into space at the speed of 130,000 miles per second relative to the people on this planet, with instructions to travel for 10 years before returning, I would, upon coming back to earth, find that I had aged 10 years while everyone and everything on earth had aged 20 years. With me traveling at that speed, 20 years of your time would transpire in 10 years of mine. If I could travel 150,000 miles per second relative to you, a thousand years of your time would be compressed into what I would experience in a day. And if I could travel at the speed of light (186,000 miles per second) then all of human history and the history of the planet itself would be compressed into a moment which has no extension of time and could properly be called "now."

An experiment conducted at the physics research laboratories of Princeton University involved studying the effects of rapid speed on a hydrogen atom set in motion in a cyclotron. The hydrogen atom traveled at speeds that approximated 32,000 miles per second. That was the highest speed at which the atom could travel while still providing scientists the possibility of observing its pulsation rate (that is, the rate at which the electron circles the nucleus of the atom). As the relative speed of the atom increased, this rate of pulsation slowed down. The speed at which the electron circled the nucleus of the atom decreased. At least, that's the way it appeared to the scientists observing this phenomenon. If the atom itself had consciousness, it would not perceive that it had slowed down, but instead would perceive that the world of the scientist had speeded up.[13]

Time is relative to motion and at the speed of light, time as an inexorable flow of successive events ceases to exist at all. At the speed of light, everything is caught up in an eternal now. The temporal is caught up in the eternal. It is difficult to pull all of this together, especially for those of us whose categories of thinking are not adapted to an Einsteinian perspective on reality. However, the more I read in the field of contemporary astrophysics, the more I am convinced that "now" is part of eternity and that eternity can be experienced now. I am led to believe that what I encounter now does not simply become part of dead history, but is part of an *eternal now* that belongs to another level of existence.

In summary, phenomenological psychology helps me to see that I live in the now, and modern astrophysics suggests to me that the now that I experience is part of an *eternal now* which gathers together the beginning and the end of all that can be called human experiences. If all of this seems "way out," I must remind you that even Einstein was not able to determine where physics ended and metaphysics began. His probing of time brought him to an awareness of an *eternal now* which encompasses all that I am and all that I will ever be.

THEOLOGICAL CONSIDERATIONS

Discussion of time, from an Einsteinian perspective, is not only useful in our efforts to try to convince the secularist that there is an eternal quality to the now of his existential being, but it is also useful in our attempts to resolve some of the dilemmas that have haunted Christian theology since the time of the early church.

The Doctrine of Predestination

One such problem revolves around the doctrine of pre-destination. Established by the writings of the Apostle Paul in the Epistle to the Ephesians, expressed and modified in the writings of St. Augustine, and given modern classical expression in the work of the reformer, John Calvin, the doctrine of predestination has threatened our belief in man's free will. Quite simply, the doctrine follows a logical progression which begins with the belief in the foreknowledge of God. According to the Calvinists, God knows everything before it happens. Because this is the case, everything that will happen is already established in the mind of God, and therefore must happen just as God knows that it will. This seems to leave room for little in the way of human freedom, and cannot be otherwise. There is strong biblical support for this position, for the Apostle Paul writes:

> For whom he did foreknow, he also did predestinate to be conformed to the image of his Son, that he might be the firstborn among many brethren. Moreover whom he did predestinate, them he also called: and whom he called, them he also justified: and whom he justified, them he also glorified.
>
> *Romans 8:29–30*

Down through the ages, many Christians have tried to reject this seemingly fatalistic doctrine that threatens to reduce human beings to actors who carry out roles that are written into a divine script before the foundation of the earth. The followers of Jacob Arminius, the Wesleyans, and a host of other Christians have argued that a person's destiny is not preordained but is determined by decisions the individual makes during his lifetime. The argument between the advocates of free will and the proponents of predestination have long split the church and brought many new denominations into being.

These two theological camps can be affirmed and reconciled when we understand the nature of time from the new perspective provided by Einsteinian physics. If God gathers together all of time in an eternal now, then with him there can be no before or after. To use biblical terminology, He is the Alpha and the Omega, the beginning and the end. With God there is no passage of time as we understand it. All things happen now

with Him. Therefore, the Calvinists are right when they say
that God knew what would happen now before the foundation
of the world, because time before the foundation of the world
and now are all the same moment with God. He knows everything as it happens and everything that happens, happens now
with Him. The Arminians are also right when they advocate
free will, because the existential moment in which a person
decides to act is part of God's eternal now. Therefore, God
knows about the decision when it occurs, not before, because
there is no before with God. This moment always was with
God, and furthermore, it always will be. Calvinists must understand that what we perceive as before or after is always
now with the Almighty One. With Him, there is no passage of
time as we know it.

This sense of the "now-ness" of God seems everywhere evident in the Scripture. The very name of God set forth by Moses
in the Book of Exodus is *Yahweh*, which means "I am that I
am." God never was, He never will be, He always is. Jesus
affirmed His deity when He said, "Before Abraham was, I am."
A statement like that is either poor grammar or evidence of a
profound truth. In this case, Jesus affirmed that He is one who
always is and never was, and hence is God. What was the
historical past for Abraham is caught up in the eternal now of
God. When Jesus declares that He experiences the time before
Abraham as the present, He is declaring Himself as Yahweh.

Between Death and the Second Coming

Another theological conflict which has divided the church
down through the ages has to do with what happens to people
between their death and the Second Coming of Christ. On the
one hand, most Christians believe that immediately upon
dying we are present with God. The Bible supports this claim,
and this promise has given hope to countless believers as they
have faced death. On the other hand, there are evangelical
Christians, like the Seventh Day Adventists, who can cite

Scripture to prove that when we die we remain in the grave until the day of the Second Advent, when those who have trusted in Christ will be physically resurrected to eternal life:

> But I would not have you to be ignorant, brethren, concerning them which are asleep, that ye sorrow not, even as others which have no hope. For if we believe that Jesus died and rose again, even so them also which sleep in Jesus will God bring with him. For this we say unto you by the word of the Lord, that we which are alive and remain unto the coming of the Lord shall not prevent them which are asleep. For the Lord himself shall descend from heaven with a shout, with the voice of the archangel, and with the trump of God: and the dead in Christ shall rise first: Then we which are alive and remain shall be caught up together with them in the clouds, to meet the Lord in the air: and so shall we ever be with the Lord.
>
> *1 Thessalonians 4:13–17*

Passages like this seem to indicate clearly that Christians who die will remain asleep until the eschaton.

Once again, what appear to be irreconcilable positions can be harmonized within the context of understanding provided by the theory of relativity. For instance, if I die January 1, 1983, and the Second Coming of Christ occurs January 1, 1993, those who live until the Second Coming of Christ will view me as one who is buried and awaiting the resurrection that will accompany the Second Advent of Christ. They would say that for ten years my body lay in the grave, decaying and turning to dust, and that when the trumpet sounds and the Lord returns, these corrupting remains will be miraculously transformed into an incorruptible body. However, when we consider the relative nature of time, we realize that the waiting period between my death and the Second Coming is only experienced by those who are caught up in the time sequence on earth. With God all things happen in the eternal now, and that means that the moment in which I die and the moment in which the Lord returns, no matter how distant in the future, are part of the instantaneous now with God and with all who are caught up to be with Him.

Once again, both sides of the argument are correct and can be synthesized into one glorious truth. On the one hand, the Adventists are right as they declare, "I will sleep until the end of historical time." On the other hand, others can rightly declare the Scripture that says "to be absent from the body is to be present with the Lord." Both are true, because with God "time shall be no more" and in heaven will be "no waiting."

The Theology of Paul Tillich

Lastly, I would like you to consider the way in which the insights of phenomenological psychology and Einsteinian physics contribute to an understanding of the theology of Paul Tillich, one of the most complex and profound of the modern existentialist theologians.[14] Tillich teaches that God cannot be known objectively. He is not a thing that exists alongside of other things. He cannot be described, nor depicted. All descriptions and portrayals of Him are idolatrous. God can only be encountered in the "now." Because He is the great "I am," I can only encounter Him by surrendering to an I-Thou relationship (as Martin Buber would call it) with Him. To be in such a relationship is what it means to be saved. Consequently, an individual can know all *about* God without knowing God. Salvation is not gained by accepting propositional truths about God's nature and powers, but rather in an event that occurs when I allow myself to become one with Him.

Many who know about Him do not know Him through such an encounter, and it may be that many who have encountered Him do not know much about Him. I once again quote Lao-tzu: "Those who know do not say, and those who say do not know." Ultimately, the purpose of evangelism is not simply to get people to accept the Church's description of God, but to call people to surrender to an I-Thou relationship with the Almighty so that they might know the eternal life that they can experience in the now.

This has not been an easy chapter to write and I am sure it must be an even more difficult chapter to read. I was tempted to cut out this material in order to create a more popular book that would be more readily understood and easily discussed. However, the insights of phenomenological psychology and Einsteinian physics seemed crucial to my attempt to develop a response to what the secularists have to say about temporality. As you probe the insights provided by phenomenological psychology and contemporary astrophysics, I am hopeful that you will discover further implications and truths that will buttress the claims of the Christian Church and help you develop a viable theology.

6.
Relativity: When Morals Become Mores

If there is no God, then anything is permissible, says Dmitri in Fyodor Dostoyevsky's classic novel *The Brothers Karamazov.* Dmitri sees that without God, man would be left to create his own values. The sense of right or "oughtness," as Immanuel Kant would call it, would no longer be a divine imperative, but the result of a socially conditioned conscience. If there were no God, man would be left to make his own laws and establish his own principles for living.

SOCIETY AS MORAL AUTHORITY

Religious skepticism led Thomas Hobbes, a British empiricist, to argue in favor of what he called "the social contract theory."[1] According to Hobbes, the only laws that govern behavior are laws that men create for themselves in order to form a society that offers to its members mutual protection. According to the "contract," each member of the society gives up his natural right to be at war with everyone, to steal from anyone, and to be controlled by no one. In exchange, each member receives the protection of the group and the benefits that are derived from living in a cooperative social system. According to Hobbes, the laws that men create in order to organize their society take precedence over the rights of the individual. Societal laws provide a determination of right and wrong that transcends the individual. Consequently, there is no ultimate right or wrong, only the right and wrong established by men in society.

The Cambodian Question

The proposition that if there is no God then the society provides the only law higher than that of the individual was clearly illustrated for me during the turbulent years that accompanied the war in Southeast Asia. President Richard M. Nixon had ordered U.S. troops into Cambodia, and consequently demonstrations and violent reactions erupted on university campuses across the nation. At that time I was teaching at the University of Pennsylvania, and the first reaction of the antiwar leaders on campus was to call a mass meeting for students and faculty. As I took my place in the crowd, I sensed the frustration and anger seething there. One by one, representatives from various campus organizations took turns speaking against the war and calling for demonstrations and political action aimed at challenging the Nixon government. One of the speakers, dressed in the typical counterculture uniform of jeans and khaki jacket, startled the crowd by asking, "How many of you believe in God?"

Someone from the crowd yelled, "What's God got to do with all of this?" "Everything," responded the speaker. "If there is no God, then the only concept of right and wrong is that which is established by society. This society has decided that it is right to kill people in the villages of Cambodia and Vietnam. If you do not agree with society's morality, then you should work to change it, or you should go to live in another society that has principles more to your liking. Personally, I do believe in God, therefore the state does not provide my highest law. The laws of God are above the laws of the state. Insofar as I can figure out, what Nixon says is right, God says is wrong. I have a higher authority than society and it is my loyalty to that higher authority that makes me an opponent of my government. If there is no God, then you have no right to say that Nixon is wrong."

Someone in the crowd mumbled something about the laws of humanity and someone else yelled at the speaker, demanding that he sit down and shut up. But what he had said had made its impact. If there is no God, then what is right and wrong is left to society to establish. If men want the benefits of society they must obey its laws. If every man in a social system feels that he has the right to create his own rules and establish his own standards of right and wrong, society would be impossible. Social chaos would reign supreme and social anomie would make human existence precarious. If a man does not agree with the laws of society he can work within the system to change them. Until they are changed he must abide by them.

The Findings of the Anthropologists

The secularist is aware of the fact that without God values and moral principles are socially relative. He realizes that from his perspective what one society establishes as right, another society might establish as wrong. Furthermore, he has the evidence of anthropologists to support this opinion. Crosscultural studies made over the last 150 years give ample evidence that what is right and wrong has to be understood in terms of the functional requisites of society. William Graham Sumner, in his monumental work, *Folkways*, makes it clear that each society establishes a morality that requires people to live by rules that will guarantee the survival of the social system.[2] Furthermore, Sumner points out that what facilitates the social well-being of one group in one geographical setting may not be good for another group in another physical setting. Many anthropologists, following this lead, tend to be moral

relativists and try to convince us that we cannot judge the
behavior of people in one society by the moral principles of
another.

Many prominent anthropologists have challenged the eth-
nocentrism that has led Western people to believe that their
moral principles and precepts are superior to those of other
people in other cultures. Margaret Mead's research among the
people in the Samoan Islands provided evidence that in this
society, outside of Christendom, people had created a lifestyle
that was less aggressive and much more loving than anything
that could be found in the Western world. Greatly impressed
by the gentleness, kindness, and love that existed among the
Samoans, Mead was forced to ask how the people of "Christian" nations could call themselves morally superior.[3]

Bronislaw Malinowski's studies of the Trobriand Islanders
raised similar challenges and questions about the claimed
moral superiority of nations in the Judeo-Christian tradition.[4]
The Trobriand Islanders developed a social system that nega-
ted the possibility of war and taught enemies to get even with
each other by outdoing one another in good works. Among the
Trobriand Islanders it was believed that the way to "hurt" an
enemy was to give more gifts of fruit and grain than he could
ever give in return. In a sense, they demonstrated the principle
of Christ whereby people are instructed to overcome evil with
good, and to do good to those who hate them.

In more recent years, anthropologists have discovered pre-
literate societies in the Philippines and in South America that
lack aggressive tendencies and whose languages do not con-
tain words for war and hate. All of this has made it abundantly
clear to the secularists that there is little basis for the claim
that the ethical principles of the Bible are superior to all other
principles as Christians so commonly claim. Furthermore, the
secularist concludes from the findings of anthropologists that
ethical principles can only be judged on the basis of how efficiently they provide guidelines for the survival and well-being
of the tribes that create them. The secularist argues that the

field research of anthropologists has proved conclusively that there are no God-given absolutes applicable to all men in all places, at all times.

Religious Pluralism

Within the American culture, this disposition to moral relativism is encouraged by our religious pluralism. From the very beginning, America was a place where people with differing religions and belief systems were welcomed and provided with freedom of conscience. Part of the American dream was to have a society in which Protestants, Catholics, Jews, Muslims, atheists and others could live together harmoniously and with mutual respect. For Americans, religion was to be a private matter, subject to the individual's conscience. Consequently, President Lyndon B. Johnson, a member of the Disciples of Christ Church, and his wife, an Episcopalian, asserted that their daughter's conversion to Roman Catholicism did not disturb them. "After all," said Ladybird Johnson, "religion is a private affair." Another president, Dwight D. Eisenhower, announced in his second inaugural address that every man should have religion, regardless of what the religion happens to be. He affirmed the popular assumption that one religion is as good as another and it does not make any difference what you believe as long as you believe something and don't bother anybody.[5]

In a pluralistic society like ours, religious leaders who make exclusionary claims for their particular theologies prove to be an embarrassment. Recently, Bailey Smith, the president of the Southern Baptist Convention, publicly said that God does not hear the prayers of Jews. He was operating on the fundamentalist belief that one must pray in the name of Jesus in order to have one's prayers heard and answered. The statement created a sensation and a scandal. Newspapers and television stations across the nation carried the report of Smith's claim. Public apologies were demanded. Jewish groups were upset because of the anti-Semitic overtones of the statement. Smith has since modified his position.

It seems un-American for any particular religious group to claim that it has absolute truth and that those who hold contrary opinions are wrong. In America, all religions are counted as equally valid and true, regardless of how contrary their theologies happen to be. Utilizing the same Bible, a host of religious groups come out with a variety of divergent and contradictory interpretations, all of which are treated by society as being equally true. Amidst such conditions, it is easy to understand why the secularist becomes cynical when an evangelical Christian says that he has access to the one and only absolute and eternal truth revealed in Scripture and applicable to everyone, everywhere, at all times. Intellectually, such a claim seems ridiculous. Within our pluralistic society it seems arrogant.

THE SOCIOLOGY OF KNOWLEDGE

Among sociologists and other intellectuals, the belief that moral systems are determined by sociological factors rather than divine revelation is gaining substantiation by developments in a new academic discipline known as the sociology of knowledge. Students in this field address themselves to the task of showing the ways in which social and economic conditions determine how people believe and think. Theologies and philosophies are viewed as thought systems generated by societies to legitimize their lifestyles and social practices. Initiated by Marx[6] and carried on by such notable sociologists as Karl Mannheim[7] and Max Scheler,[8] the proponents of the sociology of knowledge endeavor to show us that societies create ideas and moral principles rather than moral principles and ideas creating societies. These sociologists have made a science of demonstrating the origins of moral principles and convincingly demonstrate that they emerge out of socioeconomic needs rather than coming from a divine source.

Marxist Morality versus the Morality of the Bible

Marx and his followers point out that each socioeconomic class creates a morality to justify its practices. For instance, in a bourgeois capitalistic society like ours, private property is defined as a sacred right, and laissez-faire competition is described as a God-ordained instrument for achieving social progress. Contrariwise, in a communistic society, private property is viewed as an evil, and cooperation rather than competition is the basis for social improvement. According to Marxists, each socioeconomic group develops a philosophical or theological system to promote its interests, and it endeavors to promote its ideology among all members of society. Accordingly, they teach that the way in which a person views reality, understands science, interprets the Bible, and interprets justice is determined by the class to which he belongs. Marxians believe that what a person believes is right or wrong, or true or false, is the result of his class affiliation.

I claim that the Bible is an absolute authority for faith and practice. I believe that the Scriptures are a divine revelation that clearly show us what is right and wrong. I am convinced that biblical principles should guide all the peoples of the world and should be brought to bear in every culture. However, there are Marxist Christians who quickly point out that my approach is far too simplistic. The Bible has to be interpreted, they contend, and it is obvious that different people will interpret the Bible in different ways. What is important to these Marxist Christians is their belief that class identity is the major determinant of a person's interpretation of Scripture. For instance, a rich capitalist will understand the Bible one way while an impoverished proletarian communist will understand it another way. Increasingly, I find evidence to support this Marxist claim.

The Question of Affluence

A few years ago, Ronald Sider, one of my colleagues at Eastern Baptist Theological Seminary, wrote a book entitled *Rich Christians in an Age of Hunger.*[9] Sider sets forth a simple thesis that Yahweh is a God who is committed to justice for the poor. In what I believe is a brilliant exposition of Scripture, Sider shows from the Old and New Testaments that God identifies with the plight of oppressed peoples and severely judges the rich ruling classes for not responding to the needs of His people. Sider shows that throughout Scripture, whenever there are people who are suffering from economic oppression or are the victims of social injustice, God responds to their suffering by identifying with them and championing their struggle against the rich and the powerful who dominate them. His book clearly demonstrates that to be a follower of Christ is to champion the cause of justice for the poor and the downtrodden. To be a Christian is to identify with the oppressed and despised peoples of the world.

Furthermore, Sider believes that we Christians should be willing to sacrifice our possessions and our wealth so that we can help feed the hungry people of the world. He calls upon the followers of Christ to abandon the affluent lifestyle characteristic of Americans. He believes that the Bible teaches us that we should live simply and use our surplus wealth to alleviate the sufferings of the poor people of the world. He simply suggests that Jesus meant it when He said, "It is easier for a camel to go through the eye of a needle than for a rich man to enter into the Kingdom of God." He believes the churches would be more consistent with Scripture if they turned from spending billions of dollars on buildings and sanctuaries and used the money to feed the hungry and to develop economic programs that would deliver the poor from their suffering conditions.

The reaction to Sider's book has troubled me greatly. People
in upper-middle class churches write Sider off as a Marxist
(which I personally know is not true). They contend that when
Jesus says that those who would be His disciples must sell
what they have and give to the poor, He only means that people should get their priorities straightened out. These middle-
class critics of Sider like to point out that in the Old Testament
Abraham was a very rich man and so was Job, and yet they had
favor in the eyes of God. Some even go so far as to argue that
the reason people are poor is not that they are the victims of
injustice but that they do not live according to the teachings of
God's Word. Therefore, they contend, poverty can only be
eliminated by getting people saved, and we should concen-
trate on this task rather than talk about the redistribution of
wealth.

As I listen to the attempts to justify the wealth of rich Christians, it becomes increasingly clear to me that these upper-
middle class critics of Sider have chosen to interpret the
Scripture in a way that allows them to remain comfortable in
their riches in a world beset with hunger and poverty. Their
interpretation of the Bible leaves them feeling justified in
their affluent lifestyles and enables them to reduce the Scriptures to a message about individualistic salvation that does
little to disturb the socioeconomic status quo. When Scriptures are so handled, Marxist Christians can easily substanti-
ate their claim that the Bible is not taken at face value by
most church people, but rather it is reinterpreted to support
the social and economic interests of the ruling class.

"Liberation Theology"

Marxist Christians have become very prominent among the
churches of Latin America. Propagating what they call "liberation theology," such men as Jose Miquez Bonino,[10] Rubem
Alves,[11] Juan Luis Segundo,[12] Camilo Torres,[13] and Gustavo
Gutierrez[14] have become major theologians whose writings

are given serious consideration by intellectuals throughout the world. The liberation theologians claim that the Bible was written by the oppressed and for the oppressed. They point out that Jesus Himself was born to an oppressed people and lived out His life as a poor man among poor men. His disciples were likewise drawn from the working class, and the Bible itself points out that Christianity was a movement that brought together the poor, the uneducated, and the powerless to form a movement that would bring to naught the power, wealth, and knowledge of the ruling class. According to the proponents of liberation theology, only by possessing the consciousness of an oppressed people can one approach the Scripture equipped to interpret it properly.

In North America, liberation theology has its best expression in the works of the black theologian James Cone.[15] In a way that shocks middle-class sensitivities, Cone declares that only "niggers" understand the Bible because it was for them that it was written. When Cone uses the term "nigger" he is not referring to a racial class, but to a socioeconomic group of people who are despised and rejected by the mainstream of society. It is his contention that Jesus was a "nigger" and that anyone who would follow Jesus must become a "nigger" too.

THE ROLE OF THE CHURCH

When taken together, the discoveries of anthropologists, the religious pluralism of America, and the insights provided by the sociology of knowledge seem to give all the justification that is necessary for the secularist to contend that all values are relative and that every moral system is viable only for the group that creates it. It is easy to see why he considers people like me narrow-minded and even bigoted when we claim that we possess a means to discover absolute and universal moral principles. But that is exactly what we do. We claim that the Bible is a repository of truth from which we can deduce a universally valid ethical system. We take the Bible very seriously, and, in spite of the higher and lower biblical criticism that was born in nineteenth-century Germany, we still hold the Bible to be an infallible revelation from God.

In order to avoid the accusation that there are as many interpretations of Scripture as there are interpreters, it is necessary for Christians to develop a strong theology of the Church. Unfortunately, evangelicals have tended to reduce Christianity to an individualistic experience and have minimized the importance of their corporate affiliation as the Body of Christ. For most of them, the Church is a gathering of people who come together to study the Bible, to pray, and to evangelize. They do not view the Church as possessing any mystical qualities or supernatural powers. Consequently, they fail to understand the significant role the Church can play in the process of interpreting Scripture.

The Perils of Subjective Scripture Interpretation

Karl Barth, the dominating figure of twentieth-century theology, may have hurt us all by failing to understand the role of the Church in the process of interpreting Scripture.[16] He taught his followers to believe that as the individual reads Scripture, the Holy Spirit enables him to perceive what God wants him to see. According to Barth, when the individual is possessed by the Holy Spirit while reading the Scripture, the Scripture becomes the Word of God. The problem that I see in Barth's theology of revelation is that the whole thing becomes too private and dependent upon what the individual experiences. There may come a time when the individual experiences nothing, senses no divine presence, and even doubts that what he thought were revelations in the past were genuine and valid. When the condition of revelation is tied up with the spiritual state of the individual, his access to truth is established on very precarious grounds.

One of Barth's followers, William Hamilton, is an example

of the dangers inherent in the Barthian method of appropriating the revelation of God. He explains to his readers that for years he taught that under the influence of the Spirit, he sensed God speaking to him as he read the Scriptures. Then one day, he had the courage to face up to the reality that he really was not experiencing what he said he was experiencing, and that he had only been kidding himself when he claimed that God spoke to him as he read the Scriptures. His neo-orthodoxy came tumbling down and Hamilton became one of the prime spokesmen of the "God is Dead" movement.[17]

Recently, some of the most prominent evangelical leaders have advocated a reexamination of the theology of the Church. They insist that individual Christians should not assume that they are entitled to private interpretations of what the Bible teaches. They point out that since the time of Christ, Christians have struggled with the meaning of Scripture and have reached a consensus on what constitutes valid interpretations of the biblical writings. This consensus is known as the tradition of the Church. The individual Christian cannot ignore this historical consensus of Christendom and establish an interpretation to his own liking, believing that his interpretation has as much validity as that presented by the Church. These evangelical leaders believe that the tradition of Christendom should guide the individual Christian as he tries to understand the ramifications of the biblical message and the way in which the teachings of Scripture apply to his existential situation. Led by Thomas Howard, these contemporary theologians encourage the evangelical community to view the Church as the Body of Christ. As such it possesses a mystical quality and a supernatural authority. When Christians are gathered together in the name of Jesus and corporately seek His will, it is believed that the Holy Spirit becomes a dynamic presence in their midst.

For Howard and like-minded theologians, the Church is more than a gathering. It is an event in which Christ Himself becomes a controlling presence guiding and directing the thought processes and decision-making of the group. They believe that when the body of believers is prayerfully submissive to the Holy Spirit, something miraculous happens. The Holy Spirit creates a unified consciousness among the members, and that unified consciousness is believed to be the will of God. As the body of believers prayerfully seeks God's truth while interpreting the Scripture, they will know that they have reached it when they are of one accord in their understanding of the meaning of the biblical revelation at any given point.

The Leading of the Holy Spirit

These evangelical theologians point out that in the life of the early Church, believers were convinced they had discerned the will of God when they were "altogether and of one accord." There was always room for private interpretation of Scripture, but the private interpretation was subject to the approval of the body of believers. If the Church declared the interpretation of a particular individual out of keeping with what it believed to be the truth, then that individual was expected to surrender his viewpoints and be subject to the authority of the body of believers. Today's evangelical promoters of a strong theology of the Church assert that the mystical presence of Christ, which is experienced when Christians prayerfully come together to discern the meaning of Scripture, guides them in their interpretations and delivers them from the necessity of having to resort to individualistic interpretations which can be overly subjective.

The neo-Catholic evangelicals, as they are sometimes called, who follow the lead of Howard offer a safeguard alternative to the perils of subjectivism that seem all too obvious in the Barthian system. Their position provides deliverance from the endless debate over the inerrancy of Scripture which seems always to take place when conservative theologians get together for discussion. It is no longer necessary to argue whether or not every jot and tittle of the contemporary manuscripts were inerrantly dictated by God. For these neo-Catholic evangelicals the message from Yahweh is not simply delivered on parchment for men to read individually, but rather can be discerned by the interpretation of Scripture when the body of believers prayerfully comes together to seek the knowledge and will of God.

I must admit that these evangelical theologians, with their lofty view of the powers of the Church, seem very attractive to me. If they are right, then I am delivered from the fear that the Scriptures are being interpreted with cultural or social class biases. Their theology leaves the interpretation of Scripture to the leading of the Holy Spirit, who transcends all cultures and classes and is the living Word of God in our age. What God wants us to know can be learned and understood as I become a part of the Body of Christ, which possesses the ability to discern His message.

There is only one real problem with all of this ecclesiastical theology and that is that there is no way of proving that it is true. Neither logic nor empirical research can establish its claims. I know that books on Christian apologetics are supposed to present "evidence that demands a verdict." But, while this theology of the Church makes sense to me, there is no way in which I can validate it for a skeptical secularist. In my own life, I try to practice what this theology preaches. I will not accept a private interpretation of the Bible as valid if it stands in opposition to the tradition of Christendom and fails to gain confirmation from the body of believers.

THE UNIVERSALITY OF MORAL SYSTEMS

I have tried to set forth existentially how I seek truth and why I believe that my method of discovering it delivers me from the socioeconomic influences that secularists believe make all truth and knowledge relative. However, I do not want to end the matter there. Even if my theology makes no sense to the secularists, there are other reasons why their premises about the relative nature of truth and values should be called to question. There is good reason to believe that moral precepts and ethical teachings are not as relativistic as many of the secularist mentors in the field of cultural anthropology might suppose.

Another Look at the Realities

I would challenge the secularist to reevaluate his crosscultural studies, because I believe he will discern that among the peoples of the world, there seems to be an emerging consensus of what is moral and what is right. For instance, when Abraham Maslow describes the traits and characteristics of a self-actualized human being, he articulates a value system that has wide acceptance throughout the world.[18] He finds confirmation for his values in the teachings of Buddha, the writings of Lao-tzu, and the Koran of Mohammed, as well as in the Judeo-Christian Scriptures. When the secularist writer describes human beings as seeking self-actualization by first meeting the basic physical needs of existence and then moving on to find ultimate fulfillment in altruistic self-giving to others, he describes a value system that gains universal confirmation. Even people in Marxist nations who declare themselves the enemies of religion affirm the belief that humanity was designed for loving and giving and helping. When Erich Fromm, a neo-Marxist psychologist, set forth his value system and morality in his book *The Art of Loving*, Christians greeted his message with enthusiasm.[19] Fromm said, without reference to God, what many Christians had tried to say about love and faith. The secularist may be forced to admit that if he were to assemble in one room the representatives of various societies espousing different philosophies and religions and ask them to define what it means to be a fulfilled or actualized human being, he would find a much higher level of agreement among those people than his theories about the relativity of values would have ever led him to suspect.

Whenever the representatives of the United Nations meet in New York, I am amazed at the unanimity of opinion about what is right and what is wrong that exists among them. It is with a singular value system that racism is condemned, sexism questioned, and dehumanization opposed. A careful reading of the United Nations charter will clearly show that a common ethical value system is universally encouraged. I am not suggesting that all of the nations of the world live up to that ethical system. I am only pointing out that they recognize that all of their actions must be justified in accord with the principles set forth in the U.N. charter. The fact that people do not behave the right way does not mean that they do not acknowledge a universal basis for establishing what is right and wrong. Perhaps cultural anthropologists have become so enamored with exotically peculiar cultures that they fail to see what is generally true for the human race. They may not see the forest because of the trees. They may fail to see that undergirding the vast differences that exist between peoples there is a common understanding of what constitutes human dignity and social justice.

Natural Revelation

As an evangelical Christian, I do not claim that only those in the Judeo-Christian tradition have an understanding of the absolutes of good and evil. The Bible teaches that there is a natural revelation available to all people everywhere. It is to this natural and universal revelation of values and morality that the Apostle Paul refers in the first chapter of his Epistle to the Romans:

Because that which may be known of God is manifest in them; for God hath shown it unto them. For the invisible things of him from the creation of the world are clearly seen, being understood by the things that are made, even his eternal power and Godhead; so that they are without excuse.

Romans 1:19–20

The Perfection of Jesus Christ

On the other hand, I do affirm that the ethical precepts with which all peoples and religions grapple have their fullest expression in the life of Jesus Christ and can be known in perfected form only in Him. Furthermore, I believe that while all people and religions struggle toward a common understanding of what it means to be a self-actualized human being, Christ alone provides the way through which that fullness of humanity can be achieved. He provides the way to achieve the humanity that the peoples of the world crave with an insatiable appetite. There is a universal awareness of what we should become, but He alone is the way, the truth, and the life.

III
WHERE DO WE FIND GOD?

7.

A Theology for Secular Man

Sigmund Freud once commented that the Church social-
izes its youth to ask only those questions the Church is able to
answer. Any questions that it cannot adequately handle are
made to seem ridiculous. By the time the children come of age,
the Church seems to have the answer to all the important
questions of life, because the Church has taught them which
questions to ask and which questions should not be asked.

It's a simple but clever system. It helps us to understand why
people who are in the Church think it has all the answers to all
the questions and problems that are important, while those
who are outside the Church feel that it has nothing to say about
the things that are really important. If you want to know
whether the Second Coming of Christ will come before or after
the millennium, you can hear whole sermons on the subject. If
what concerns you is whether once you are a Christian you can
ever lose your salvation, you will find theologians who have
written books on the subject. Perhaps you are concerned about
speaking in tongues and want to know how to secure a "second
blessing" that will enable you to possess the gift of *glossolalia*.
Simply turn on your TV set—there is bound to be an "electric
church" evangelist who will be able to tell you how you too can

speak in a heavenly language. Of course, such questions may
not be important to you and the answers to them may be no
concern of yours. In that case, the preaching of the Church will
all seem like foolishness. But after all, say some of the defend-
ers of ecclesiastical thought, the preaching of the Church has
always seemed like foolishness to the world. Isn't that what
the Bible itself teaches?

RESPONDING TO REAL QUESTIONS

Too often, the people of the Church fail to see what Paul
Tillich called "the theological circle."[1] According to Tillich,
the place of the Church is not to raise questions, but to attempt
to provide answers. The Church should step aside and let the
people of the world raise the questions. The Church should be a
listening body—sensitive to the deepest concerns of the
world's peoples, intently interested in their problems, struggling to provide solutions to their most troublesome inquiries,
and endeavoring always to serve as their servant. It's all too
easy for the people of the Church to say, "We've got the answers," without having first inquired as to what the questions
might be.

I often find myself guilty of this tendency not to listen to the
world, whom I readily criticize. All too frequently I have prepared sermons, delivered messages, and preached what I believed to be the truth, without seriously asking about the
needs and concerns of my listeners. For that reason, I now
consider it providential that in 1965 I suddenly and unexpect-
edly found myself thrust into the role of a sociology professor
at the University of Pennsylvania. In lectures and seminars, I
was confronted time and time again by bright and earnest
students who would not allow me the luxury of dealing with
my questions, but instead demanded that we discuss theirs.
In after-class discussions that often ran until two o'clock in
the morning, they interrogated me to see if I had anything to
say about the things that concerned them. For the first time, I

had to develop a theology that answered their questions, instead of the ones with which I had become so familiar in seminary.

Above the din of the many voices, there was one question that was clearly sounded again and again. My secular friends and colleagues wanted to know what it means to be human and how humanness can be achieved. There were other questions that in one way or another all seemed to be related to this dominant one. My questioners' cries for social justice expressed a hope that there might be a world in which every person could have the privilege of actualizing his humanity. Their studies in psychology seemed to focus on discovering the way to become fully human. Even their experimentation with LSD and other drugs revealed a desire to heighten awareness so that life might be appreciated in greater depths and a full humanness might be enjoyed.

The seekers seemed to gravitate to the social scientists rather than to the philosophers. At first, I couldn't understand this, but when I gained a sense of what philosophy was about at my university, I understood. Many of those in the philosophy department fit the description of modern philosophers which Thomas Merton, the Trappist monk, provided: "Having nothing to say they concentrated on the art of saying nothing with exactness." Philosophy seemed to be an exercise in linguistic analysis and mathematical formulations. There were courses in the works of Ludwig Wittgenstein and Rudolf Carnap, which helped the students to develop a language style freed from emotional and religious overtones that could adequately describe the realities of the empirical world. While philosophers in other ages made significant statements that we were never sure were true, their modern counterparts confined themselves to making statements that were true and had no significance. The fact that any statement that could not be tested by their verification principle was declared meaningless, left very little in human discourse that could be said to have any meaning at all.

No wonder the students turned away from modern philosophy and looked for hope in the courses of psychology and sociology. It is interesting to note that in the late 1960s, I was offering the only course in existentialism available in that large university. Students who wanted to find out about love, intimacy, and humanization were attracted to courses in humanistic psychology. Erich Fromm, Ashley Montagu, Viktor Frankl, and Abraham Maslow seemed to offer more meaningful answers to their questions than those philosophers who had made it their express business to make "meaningful" statements. The works of Norman O. Brown and R. D. Laing had greater attraction than the logical positivism of Antony Flew or the products of that group of philosophers called the Vienna Circle.

It was in the ferment and excitement of such a setting that I had to rework what I believed, in order to give Christian answers to the questions that burned in the hearts and minds of my students. I found that my restructured theology often helped my secular friends and colleagues, and much to my surprise, some of them were converted to the Christian faith. It was not long before members of my own department began to grumble about what I was saying and doing in class, contending that I had taken my courses and turned them into evangelistic church services. As I look back on what was going on in those exciting days, I must confess that they were probably right. However, the fact that students listened with intense interest to what the Bible has to say about the human condition as they perceived it convinced me that we need not be ashamed of the gospel of Christ. The message of Jesus does provide answers, but first we must listen to the questions.

TOWARD A PERSONAL THEOLOGY

Late one Thursday afternoon my seminar class had reached that time of day when one can normally expect students to be a bit drowsy, longing for the end of the classroom period. However, when I asked them what it was they wanted out of life, the class immediately came alive.

"I want to become human—fully human," one of my students blurted out. He stood up, which was unusual behavior in the informal setting of the seminar room. "We all want to be human," he said. "We don't know how to become human and nothing that I've heard in this class up to this point has provided any hints."

"What do you mean by 'human'?" I inquired. "Can you describe the traits of humanness? Can you list the characteristics of humanness? Can you give me some idea of what it is you want to achieve? After all, how can I tell you how to become human when you have not told me what humanness is?"

"Come off it," he said. "Everybody knows what it means to be human! It means to be loving, infinitely loving; sensitive, infinitely sensitive; aware, totally aware; empathetic, completely empathetic; forgiving, graciously forgiving. I could go on, but I would only be elaborating on the obvious. Everyone here knows what I am talking about when I say 'humanness,' and you do too, so stop putting me on."

"O.K.," I said. "I was putting you on. I do know what you mean by humanness. But I must probe a bit further. You know something of love, something of empathy, something of forgiveness. Even if you possess these traits to a very limited degree, you obtained them somehow. Were you born with them? Were they part of your biological makeup? The limited humanity that one senses in your personhood—whence did it come? What was its source?"

"You're putting me on again!" he shouted angrily. "This is a sociology class and you're a sociologist. You know that whatever qualities of humanness I possess are obtained by the process of socialization. If I am forgiving, it is because I associated with forgiving people and took on their traits and likeness. If I possess a sense of awareness to life, it is only because I interacted with people who lived in this way. If there is any love in me, it is because I have been loved by others. You know all that, so what are you trying to do?"

"What I am trying to do," I responded, "is to drive you back to a simple definition of socialization you learned in the introductory course. Remember how the textbook said, 'Socialization is the process whereby a *Homo sapiens* becomes human'? Do you remember, we explained to you that if at the moment of birth you were separated from all human beings and raised by wolves in a forest, twenty years later you would possess none of those traits that you have so eloquently suggested are evidence of humanness.

"Without human interaction you would have no language with which to think. You would have no categories with which to interpret reality. All the traits that you listed in your attempt to describe humanness to me would be lacking. You would not even have a consciousness of self, for without social relationships you would never develop the reflective capacities that are essential for self-awareness. It is only by adopting the perspective of a significant other that you become conscious that you are an existing person. In short, without interaction with human beings you would have the form of a man, but none of the traits. Your humanity is a gift of society. You become what the people who socialize you are."

"What are you trying to prove?" he asked. "Are you telling me that society makes me human? I feel just the opposite. I feel that society is dehumanizing me. It leaves me feeling alienated and unloved. It reduces me to a thing; it doesn't make me into a person."

I was setting him up for the proclamation of the Gospel. "Look," I said, "what I'm trying to tell you is that the traits of humanness are gained by associating with someone who possesses them. If you have an intimate and sustained interactive relationship with somebody who is very loving, you will become loving too. You know this from your own experience. Haven't you ever been with someone who was so human that when your time with him was over, you felt your humanity had been enhanced, enlivened, and raised to a higher level? What I am trying to explain is that you will become as human as the person who becomes the significant other in your life, the one to whom you relate most intimately. Of course, if there is no such person, you will never become fully human and you will probably lose what little humanity you presently possess."

"But you don't understand," he responded. "If I want to be fully human, if I want to be the totally actualized person that Abraham Maslow asks me to be, if I am to become everything that I potentially am, I must have a relationship with somebody like that. I don't know anybody like that. What's more, I doubt if there is anybody like that. If I can only become as human as the most significant person I relate to, then I can never become fully human, because there is no one I can relate to who has achieved this state of being."

It was a perfect set-up and I think he knew it. I believe he anticipated what I was about to say.

"Yes, there is," I responded. "His name is Jesus. Read the New Testament. Read it honestly and openly. Read the four Gospels specifically. Learn about Jesus, and, as you learn about Him, ask a very simple question: doesn't Jesus possess the fullness of humanity? Isn't He infinitely loving, graciously forgiving, totally empathetic, and infinitely aware of people in the world in which He lives?

"You might ask how someone who lived two thousand years ago can answer your need for a humanizing relationship here and now. But you know my answer. You know that I am convinced that the Jesus described in the New Testament is resurrected from the grave, is present here and now, and invites you into the kind of relationship that holds your only hope for becoming what He is. You will probably say that the bad news is that He doesn't really exist, but I am trying to declare the good news that He really does. He wants to be personally related to you and He wants you to allow Him to transform you into His likeness."

Surprisingly, he and the other students of my class were fascinated. They had all heard about the Jesus who died on the cross to save them from hell. They knew about the Jesus who was the enemy of the devil. From radio preachers they had learned that if you believe in Jesus, you might get rich or be healed of rheumatism. But they had never heard about a Jesus who humanizes. We were suddenly talking about Jesus in another way that just might provide an answer to the urgent question that had initiated the discussion.

The class hour came to an end, but my students didn't want to stop the discussion. One of them invited the class over to his apartment so that we might discuss the matter more fully, and after a quick telephone call home to excuse myself from dinner, I accepted the invitation, not realizing that the discussion would keep me going until after midnight. It was that discussion which initiated the restructuring of my theology in order that I might be able to address in some way the question that was urgently asked by my secular friend.

THE CHRISTIAN MEANING OF BEING HUMAN

I must have heard a hundred talks by evangelical preachers who argue that humanism is the greatest threat that Christianity has ever had to face. Members of theologically conservative "God squads" have mobilized for the war against humanistic philosophy which they believe is rearing its ugly head everywhere. Fundamentalist colleges find it easy to raise the necessary funds to stay in business simply by telling unsuspecting church people that "Christian education" is a last bulwark against the humanistic barbarian hordes that are beating on the gates of their religious empires. There are television preachers who rile against humanism, and a variety of religious films to be shown at Sunday evening church services, featuring "Christian scholar" types who warn that humanism will get the best of us in these "last days."

With all of this noise and fury, it is difficult to say anything good about humanism, but that is exactly what I intend to do. I think the Gospel is about becoming human. I think that Jesus came into the world primarily to deliver us from our dehumanizing behavior and tendencies, and to make us into the human beings that He willed for us to be when He created us. I think that being saved is realizing our potentiality for humanness rather than becoming otherworldly persons who find being *Homo sapiens* a real drag. In short, I believe that Christianity is about achieving humanity and is built on the premise that true humanness can only come through an intimate relationship with Christ. The theology that I developed in the context of discussions with my secularist friends can properly be labeled "Christian humanism" and affirms that the achieving of the fullness of humanity is the ultimate end of all things and ultimately the will of God. What follows is an elaboration of that theology and a continuation of the discussion which began in my class in existentialism.

I will relate this discussion to you as though I had tape-recorded it. In reality I am composing the dialogue from my recollections. Needless to say, I come out looking better and smarter than I really was in our give-and-take argument. Furthermore, my student is portrayed as one who is easily trapped and led by the expertise of his preacher/teacher. Neither was the case; there were many times in the real discussion when he got the best of me and raised a lot of questions which I could not answer. But, all in all, good things happened from our intellectual exchanges, and in the end my student friend did become a Christian. He became open to the Holy Spirit partly because the theology that emerged out of our dialogue seemed to him to be the most viable option for achieving the fullness of humanity which was so important to him.

The conversation that had started with such intensity in the seminar classroom continued that evening in the apartment my earnest secular friend and his buddies called "home." All of us were pumped up on an artificial high created from an overdose of coffee and candy bars. Anxious to get the discussion going again, I reviewed the ground we had covered.

"Back in class you listed some of the characteristics of humanness. You told us that being human was being loving, forgiving, empathetic, aware, and a whole lot of other things. You and I both know that you could have gone on indefinitely listing the traits of humanness, and after you had exhausted all the words the English language makes available for such a description, you would not have said all that could be said about what it means to be fully human. As I listen to you list the traits of humanness, something inside me seems to say that not only are you describing the self-actualized man, you are describing what God is like. God is all the things that you are telling me you want to be. Then it hit me—humanness and Godness are one and the same. You want to be conformed to the image of God—you want to be everything that Jesus was and is. What you call being human is really being Godlike."

At first this style of thinking seemed blasphemous, but before I could dismiss the idea, a host of Bible verses flowed into my consciousness, and I began to realize that what I was thinking was not at all a contradiction to what the Bible was saying. In the first chapter of John, the twelfth verse, we are told that if we have a relationship with Jesus Christ we will become "sons of God." And the same thing is written by the Apostle Paul in the eighth chapter of Romans, verses 15–17:

> For ye have not received the spirit of bondage again to fear; but ye have received the Spirit of adoption, whereby we cry, Abba, Father. The Holy Spirit itself beareth witness with our spirit, that we are the children of God; and if children, then heirs; heirs of God, and joint-heirs with Christ; if so be that we suffer with him, that we may be also glorified together.

Paul seems to be telling us that because of what happened to us in our relationship with Christ we are formed into people whose relationship with God allows us to address Him as "Abba" (equivalent to our word *daddy*). However, it seemed clear to me that if I surrender to such a relationship with

Christ, and become like Him, I would possess all the traits and qualities that my student called human.

My student was beginning to grasp my line of thinking. He was not convinced that I was right but, nevertheless, was able to understand that what I was saying had some interesting implications. He said, "If Godness is humanness and vice versa—then we have to have a new way of talking about Jesus. Jesus is God *because* He is fully human, not in spite of His humanness. When I was a kid growing up in Sunday school, they always made it seem weird to me that God could be a man, but if I follow what you are saying it is the most logical thing in the world. Jesus was God *because* He was fully human and he was fully human *because* He was God. I had always been led to believe that becoming human was some kind of temporary and terrible condition that Jesus had to endure for a few years in order to communicate with us in a form that we could understand. But if you are right, His humanity was the fullest expression of His deity. In Jesus, everything that God *is* was revealed and everything that a human being is supposed to be was fully realized and both of these were one and the same. Jesus was not God in spite of the fact that He was human; He was God because He was human; and He was the only human that ever lived."

"That's right," I chimed in, "each of the rest of us is *Homo sapiens* in the process of becoming human. Only He is the fullness of what we aspire to become. Only He possesses the qualities of self-actualization which you said had ultimate importance for your life. When you become like Him, you not only become human, you become like God. I think this is what the Bible means when it says in the eighth chapter of Romans that we are creatures who are 'groaning' as we long for our self-realization as sons of God. When we become like Jesus we do not become pious persons with holier-than-thou dispositions. Instead we become people who manifest the 'fruits of the Spirit,' which in reality are the qualities of humanness. The

Bible says: 'But the fruit of the Spirit is love, joy, peace, patience, kindness, goodness, faithfulness, gentleness, self-control . . .' " (Gal. 5:22, 23).

My friend was now enthusiastically involved in the discussion, working intensely to spell out more of the implications of our developing theology. "What we are dealing with here leads us to an understanding of goodness and evil that is very different from what I've been taught. I had been made to believe that a person was good when he obeyed the set of rules that God had dictated in the Bible and that a person was evil when he disobeyed those laws. Now we can talk about goodness as anything that enhances the humanity of the individual and evil as anything that diminishes it. For instance, the evil of hating somebody is that my humanity would be diminished, which is another way of saying that I would become less like Jesus. On the other hand, good is doing something that helps someone else become more human and, in the process, becoming more human myself."

"You are really onto something," I shot back. "You make it clear that sin is tied up in social interaction. You are helping me to see that I cannot realize my higher potentialities of humanness without engaging in the kind of activities that humanize other people, and that the dehumanization of other people causes me to lose the image of God. If we follow that line of thinking, then something like racism is wrong because it leads to treating some people as less than human and, hence, diminishes the humanity of both the victim of racism and the practitioner of it. Sin will be viewed as something different from simply breaking some celestial laws. It also will include any behavior that robs another person of his dignity or sense of self-worth. Sin may be the *way* I talk to a person, the manner in which I look at people, and the style of my involvement with those who are part of my social intercourse. I can see that a job that leaves a person emotionally dead and physically dissipated is sinful because it diminishes that person's humanity and leaves him emotionally dead."

I was beginning to see how superficial my understanding of sin had been. As a case in point, I had always figured that the sins of the flesh were merely desires and practices of sexual relations outside of marriage. I had assumed that if you did "it" with the right person, following the proper ecclesiastical ritual, that sex was good, and that if these requisites had not been met, then "it" was evil. Now I was beginning to see that the sexual act between husband and wife could be very evil if it left either of the partners dehumanized and cheapened. Too often marital partners use each other as things and get their gratification out of reducing their partners into erotic machines. Too often sleeping together is merely a way of diminishing libidinal urges and is devoid of any concern to express a humanly enhancing kind of love. If such is the case, the religiously prescribed rules of marriage are being obeyed even while a horrendous sin is being committed. To use Martin Buber's terminology, the other person is treated as an "it" rather than as a "thou." He or she is seen as an object rather than as a sacred presence.

My student, who had been very enamored of Marxist thought, began to explain to me how this concept of sin could be reconciled with what Karl Marx had said about alienation. "Marx, particularly in his early writings, was greatly concerned about the ways in which the processes of production, which had come to characterize modern industry, left workers dehumanized. Alienation, according to Marx, was the loss of the sense of emotional oneness which should exist between the worker and what he creates. For instance, when a child makes something at school for his mother, the thing that he makes is more than a thing. In some way the child joyfully expresses himself in what he is producing. His product is an extension of who he is and what he feels. He brings it home and gives it to his mother and usually she recognizes that it is more than just an object and treats it with reverence. As the mother smiles benevolently, the child's joy knows no bounds. What he has made and how it has been received creates such ecstatic joy that his humanness has been enhanced and he has become more self-actualized.

"Whenever work fails to offer this kind of childlike excitement, it is dehumanizing. Whenever it fails to give to the worker a chance to expand his humanity through creative production, something sacred is lost. According to Marx, the means of production must allow the worker to gain emotional fulfillment in what he makes and what he does. I think our new theology has a lot in common with this Marxian thesis. Work that leaves the worker alienated is sin, and work that leaves the worker emotionally alive because of its creative nature is righteousness."

"Perhaps Marx wasn't far from the Kingdom of God," I responded. "His ideas about creativity in work as a humanizing force may have more theological meaning than he could have imagined. God is a creator, and to be creative is to be in His image. Creative work humanizes us and makes us more Godlike. We express the nature of God whenever we do things and make things that express and expand creativity."

I was beginning to see that we were saying many things that were very close to the theology of Paul Tillich, who defined sin as estrangement. Tillich argued that man in his earliest state of existence was in a state of oneness with his world, and with all that was in the world. He did not treat trees and animals as things but viewed them as persons that could be talked to and loved and even exert an influence on the lives of people. In the personalistic exchanges that characterized man's relationship with his physical environment, he found that his humanity was enhanced and his spiritual aliveness engendered. However, as man adopted a scientific orientation to his world, he lost his personal disposition to mountains and trees and animals. They all became things—objects—its. He no longer related to them in a way that enhanced his humanness and, in a sense, awakened a quality of humanness in the creatures of the physical world.

The Bible talks about the spiritual tie between man and

nature that existed prior to the Fall. Sin, points out Tillich, has broken that tie and left man estranged from nature, cut off from the gratification that could be derived from intimate fellowship with animals, flowers, trees, and mountains. It becomes hard for man to understand a St. Francis of Assisi who could talk to the birds. He finds it hard to believe in a Jesus who could speak to the wind and the waves and have them obey Him.

For estranged modern man, emotionally and psychically cut off from the creatures of his environment, there is a sense of aloneness about life in this world. He sees no potentialities for the enhancing of his humanness as he stands amidst the splendor of nature. The birds sing in a minor key for him. As he walks amongst the trees he usually experiences a kind of melancholia that seems to hint that there was once a better day when a different kind of love existed between man and what he has come to view as an environment made up of nonpersonal creatures. I have felt this tremendous sense of loss when I have been on nature outings. I must attest to the fact that a strange sadness overtakes me as I sense my "otherness" in respect to the natural beauty that surrounds me.

Tillich goes on to point out that being estranged from the creatures of nature is only one aspect of our condition of estrangement. Man, who treats animals and trees as things, gradually comes to view every other *Homo sapiens* the same way. People become things to him. He comes to view them as objects to be manipulated rather than persons to be loved. In so doing, he finds himself cut off from people, and he experiences a loneliness from which there is no escape. He craves oneness with others but doesn't know how to achieve it. The more he is with people the more he senses his estranged condition. In Sartrian fashion, he views being with other people as hell. Their mere presence mocks him, for they are so physically close and yet so distant at exactly the same moment, and he feels that there is no deliverance from this state of separateness.

My student found it easy to relate to the description of sin that we were discussing. His sophisticated education had acquainted him with art forms that gave ample testimony to this perspective. From T. S. Eliot's Wasteland to Pablo Picasso's Guernica, he had grappled with the theme of estrangement and alienation. The plays of Franz Kafka had brilliantly communicated to him the psychic and emotional poverty that comes from being a powerless person in a society that has no meaning. The works of Arthur Miller had taught him much about man's alienation in a world that neither understands him nor is understood by him.

The popular music he had played on his stereo carried the same message. John Lennon's song about Eleanor Rigby had expressed the emptiness of teenagers who should be thrilled with life but who, in reality, are filled with despair because of the absence of meaningful relationships. Simon and Garfunkel's *Sounds of Silence* had given him adequate evidence of the breakdown of communication that has come to characterize human existence.

I explained that being saved is to be delivered from this condition of alienation. It is entering into a relationship with the ultimate Human, being transformed into His likeness and enjoying the ecstasy of full aliveness.

"Then I want to be saved," he said. "If salvation means becoming fully human, then I want it. The religion upon which I was raised conveyed the idea that being saved was being delivered from the punishment of an angry God. I was made to believe that He is out to get anybody who does not agree with the Apostles' Creed. I thought if I believed all the right things and said 'yes' to all the right questions, I would go to heaven. And if I didn't, I would go to hell. I was taught that God would burn anybody who didn't believe that He loved them. Now you're telling me that being saved isn't about heaven or hell It's about becoming human here and now. It's about entering into a process whereby my potentialities for humanness are actualized."

"I didn't say there is no afterlife," I responded. "As a matter of fact, I believe that there is a heaven. The afterlife is an essential part of my belief about humanization. I believe that the process of being humanized cannot be completed during the course of our respective lifetimes. However, we can live in the hope that we will become fully human when we are with Jesus after death. Becoming fully human is what heaven is all about. I don't know whether you can buy this last statement, but it's part of my belief system."

"I can't," he said. "I would like to believe in life after death, but that's a little bit too much for me right now. Maybe later a belief in the afterlife will make some kind of sense to me. For now I only want to talk about the meaning of salvation in *this* life."

"That's O.K.," I said. "Jesus didn't make a big deal out of heaven and hell either. He didn't tell us that He entered the world in order to get people into heaven. He said He had come 'that we might have life and have it more abundantly.' I'm sure that what He meant by that was that we might achieve the kind of humanness we've been talking about. I really believe that His purpose is to enable us to become fully human."

"All of this sounds good to me," he answered, "but there's one gigantic problem to be solved if any of this is to prove helpful. I need to know, where can I meet this Jesus? I want you to explain to me how it is possible to establish a personal relationship with this Jesus who incarnates humanness. Please don't tell me that it all happens by saying a little prayer in which I invite Jesus into my heart. I hope you haven't brought me this far only to disappoint me with the same stuff that some campus evangelist laid on me last week. Tell me how I meet this Jesus who will make me fully human. Explain to me in terms that make sense to me how I can have this humanizing relationship that will enable me to overcome the feeling of alienation that plagues my existence. Where do I meet this resurrected Jesus of yours? Where do I encounter His transforming presence?"

I sat back in the maroon stuffed sofa that was the main piece of furniture in this typical graduate student flat. The eyes of Che Guevara stared down at me from the poster that hung on the wall opposite where I was sitting. Che seemed to be asking the question too. The other students who were with us in the apartment had remained silent up to this point of the discussion, but now leaned forward, eagerly. Everything hung on the answer. Where and how could the Jesus who was fully human be encountered so that His humanizing presence might change us into the self-actualized persons we all wanted to become? Obviously, this was the most important question of all.

"He can be found exactly where He said," I answered. "He told us that He did not dwell in temples and churches that we build in His honor. Instead, He encouraged us to look for Him in one another. He said, 'You are my temples; I dwell in you.' What I am trying to say is that the Jesus who incarnated God two thousand years ago is mystically present and waiting to be discovered in every person you and I encounter. I am claiming that every one of us is a priest who can communicate Jesus to those whom we meet, and that those whom we meet are priests who can communicate Jesus to each of us. Consider the very obvious fact that all of us are aware that there is something sacred in every other person. Something about each of them makes us believe that each is of infinite value and worth. Usually we do not bother to name this sacred presence we encounter in others, but we know it is real and that it requires respect.

"According to Martin Buber, there is, in addition to those traits of another person that can be known objectively and described verbally, a quality of being that he considers transcendental. He refers to this sacred quality of the other person as 'Thou.' Buber believes that if 'I' (that transcendental dimension of *my* selfhood) surrender to an intimate oneness with 'Thou,' alienation and estrangement will be overcome and humanness will be experienced. Such a relationship is called 'I-Thou' by Buber.

"Allow me to read a description of the 'I-Thou' from Buber's book," I said. Fortunately, we were using several of Buber's works in the course I was teaching and I had a copy of the book *I and Thou* with me. I turned to a passage I knew almost from memory and read:

> The Thou encounters me by grace—it cannot be found by seeking. But that I speak the basic word to it is a deed of my whole being, is my essential deed.
>
> The Thou encounters me. But I enter into a direct relationship to it. Thus the relationship is election and electing, passive and active at once: An action of the whole being must approach passivity, for it does away with all partial actions and thus with any sense of action, which always depends on limited exertions.
>
> The basic word I-Thou can be spoken only with one's whole being. The concentration and fusion into a whole being can never be accomplished by me, can never be accomplished without me. I require a Thou to become; becoming I, I say Thou.
>
> All actual life is encounter.[2]

I continued: "Such encounters are not normative in the everyday relationships we have with each other. Usually we have what Buber calls 'I-It' relationships. In 'I-It' relationships the other person is nothing more than a thing or an object. We label him and treat him as a type. He is a student, a worker, a Democrat, or a Presbyterian. In 'I-It' relationships the other person is no longer encountered with reverence, but is reduced to a typical representative of a class of creatures who perform a particular function. The man I meet in the department store is nothing more than a salesman. The man who collects my fare on the bus is simply a bus driver. The woman who handles my legal affairs is only a lawyer. Such persons are known for the roles that they play. Their function is their identity. I confront them as though they were objects. I try to be just and kind to them, and on a good day we smile at each other politely, but our relationships go no deeper than that. A year from now I won't remember any of them.

"On the other hand, an 'I-Thou' relationship offers me far

more. 'I' become involved with 'Thou' in a way that is not
ordinary or mundane. In such a relationship, each of us surren-
ders to the other, and the two of us become one. It is only after
the relationship is over and I reflect upon it objectively that I
realize how precious and wonderful it was. When I reflect
upon the 'I-Thou' encounter, I am no longer experiencing it. It
too has become a thing, a part of my past. It has become a part
of 'me.' But even as I reflect upon the 'I-Thou' encounter, I
know that there was something sublimely special about it. I
know that the 'I-Thou' encounter had a quality that encour-
ages me to regard it with reverence. I know that it is easily
differentiated from other kinds of relationships and experiences. As I reflect upon the 'I-Thou,' I realize that in it 'I' and
'Thou' experienced shared ecstasy in which 'I' temporarily
experienced the joys of full humanness.

"Buber asks us to reflect further on what is experienced
when an 'I-Thou' occurs. He claims that in every 'I-Thou' one
senses that 'the Eternal Thou' who is Yahweh is present. He
suggests that Yahweh is not an object or thing that can be
apprehended as an 'It.' Instead God is a presence who is experienced whenever an 'I-Thou' occurs. It is for this reason that
God tells us through Scripture that 'where two or three are
gathered together in my Name, there I am in the midst of
them.' God is known in the sacred 'I-Thou' encounter with
another person. Without the other person, 'I' cannot know
God.

"God is experienced when two people become one. In Him is
the reconciliation of the alienated 'I' with the 'I' of the other.
He is known only as 'I' surrender to 'Thou' and allow the 'I-
Thou' to happen. The resurrected Jesus is present in this existential event. God refuses to be an 'It' that can be concep-
tualized or described. Instead He is known in and through
relationships, and without relationships He cannot be known.
This is the reason the Bible says that any man who says he
loves God and hates his brother is a liar. It is only in loving his
brother that a man can experience God. Ultimately Jesus can

be known only when the 'I-Thou' happens. Furthermore, it is in 'I-Thou' relationships that a person can be humanized because it is in 'I-Thou' relationships that he encounters the Jesus who incarnates the fullness of humanness.

"Many people have experienced the humanizing influence of Jesus through 'I-Thou' encounters without being aware that they are experiencing Jesus. Their 'I-Thou' encounters revealed a presence that was totally other than the cultural deity they had come to know by that name. They encountered Jesus, were transformed and humanized by Him, and yet they didn't know who He was. Jesus is the only Saviour, but not everybody who is being saved by Him is aware that He is the one who is doing the saving. He is so different from the God of the theologians and philosophers.

"The Bible tells us that there will be many surprises on Judgment Day. Many who thought they knew Jesus will be turned away because they failed to sense His presence in people who were hungry, naked or lonely. On the other hand, the Scriptures tell us that the Lord will invite many who thought they had no relationship with Him to enter into His Kingdom. He will tell them that when they loved hungry people and fed them, they were relating to Him. He will explain that when they clothed the naked, ministered to the sick and visited the lonely, they were, in every instance, doing it for Him. Jesus wasn't just talking symbolically when He said, 'Inasmuch as ye have done it unto one of the least of these my brethren, ye have done it unto me.'

"If all of this sounds somewhat mystical, let me concretize it for you by relating an experience in which I became aware that Jesus waits to be encountered in those whom the Bible names as 'the least of the brethren.'

"Several years ago I visited a small community situated near the border that separates Haiti from the Dominican Republic. Standing at the edge of the grass landing strip, I awaited the arrival of the small Piper Cub airplane that was supposed to pick me up and fly me back to the capital city. As I

stood there waiting, a woman came toward me. She was carrying her baby boy. One look at him, and I knew it would not be
long before he would be dead. His stomach was swollen and
distended, an evidence of advanced malnutrition. His hair was
rust-colored from vitamin deficiencies. His spindly arms and
legs hung limply from his semi-conscious body. I could see he
was dying. His mother held him up to me and began to plead
for me to take him. 'Don't let my baby die,' she begged. 'Please
don't let him die. Take him and make him well again. Take him
back to your country. Feed him and make him well. Please,
mister—take my baby.'

"I turned away from her, not knowing what to do or what to
say. After all, there were innumerable babies, just like this one,
all over Haiti. The problem of suffering Haitian children was
too big for me to handle. But she kept coming after me, grab-
bing at my clothes, pulling at me, pleading with me to take her
child. I kept trying to get away from her, hoping she would
leave me alone, and was relieved when the airplane that was to
transport me away from this ugly scene came into sight. As
soon as it touched down at the end of the landing strip I ran
across the field to meet it. The desperate woman with her
dying baby chased after me. She screamed hysterically, 'Don't
let my baby die! Don't let my baby die!' I got to the plane,
climbed into the cockpit, closed the plexiglas door, and told
the pilot to get moving. She caught up to the airplane and ran
alongside it. Banging on the fuselage, she screamed at me,
calling me terrible names and pleading with me to take her
child. The propeller of the plane began to spin faster, the en-
gine revved up, and the plane pulled away from her. It accelerated down the landing strip and climbed into the air. As we
circled the field, I could see her solitary figure holding the
baby.

"The pilot and I flew in silence, both visibly shaken. We had
traveled halfway back to the capital city when the meaning of
what had taken place suddenly became clear to me. I realized
whom I had left behind on that grass landing strip. That little

boy was more than a starving child; more than a statistical victim of an oppressive economic system; more than a homeless Haitian. That little boy was Jesus. When I had turned away from him, I had turned away from the eternal God who broke into history two thousand years ago in order to humanize all of mankind. I had turned my back on the Lord of history and lost an opportunity for an encounter with God. Everything that is sacred, divine, and holy had been waiting to be encountered in that small child, even as the divine once awaited discovery in the manger in Bethlehem. The resurrected Jesus was there in that infant because He is in every person. I had been invited, not simply to do something for that baby, but to establish a rapport with the ultimate Human, Jesus."

"I can't buy it," said one of the young men.

"Neither can I," said another.

But the student who had talked with me so intensely sat silent for what must have been a long minute, then said, "I'll have to think about it."

The unsaved person shies away from humanizing "I-Thou" encounters. He is afraid of them because he knows that if he acknowledges the other person as one who incarnates the Eternal Thou, he will have to surrender to him in love and become a servant of the other person. His ego and pride make him resistant to such loving surrender. He feels more comfortable treating the other person as an "It" whom he can dominate and manipulate to his own ends and purposes. He feels more comfortable exercising power over the other person and being able to control him. He does not want to see the other person as one who incarnates God because he would then find it difficult to play his games of control and domination. He is afraid to recognize the resurrected Jesus mystically present in the other person.

The unsaved may be aware that Jesus invites them to be open to divine encounters that are possibilities whenever people meet, but they are afraid of such encounters. They may

know that only by surrendering to God who can be known in
other persons can they be humanized, but they are unwilling
to trust other persons. They are afraid that being vulnerable to
other people will lead to their being exploited and hurt. Unfortunately, they often *are* exploited and hurt, and the pain that
comes from being used as a thing instead of being loved as a
person is all too frequently experienced.

The "saved" realize that this perspective is erroneous. They
know that when they "submit to one another in love," they do
not lose their identity or their humanity, but instead discover
both. They discover the truth in the words of Jesus, who said,
"Whoever seeks to save his life will lose it, but whoever is
willing to lose his life for my sake will find it." Christians are
not dismayed when people take advantage of them, for they
have learned to expect such treatment from those who do not
understand what God and salvation are all about. Christians
have been taught by Jesus that they are servants of One who
was Himself rejected, and that "the servant is not greater than
the master."

8.

What the Church Can Mean

If all Christians ever experienced were the dehumanizing effects of people who use them as things, their humanity would be diminished and they would not be able to endure. Fortunately, God has called those who have responded to the good news to form a corporate body which is the Church. The members of this Christian fellowship are instructed to gather together with great regularity because the relationships they have with each other will renew them and give them back in abundance what the world threatens to take away. Within the Church, believers find an openness to love, mutual submissiveness, and the kind of "I-Thou" encounters that make them like Jesus. The world may diminish the image of God in Christians as it treats them without reverence and humiliates them with ridicule. But what the world diminishes, the fellowship of believers enhances.

The Church not only equips Christians to resist the tendencies to be dehumanized by the world; it also prepares them to conquer the deadness of the unsaved with a transforming love. They believe that as they continue to encounter people as Christ did, there will be some who will respond to their openness and who will take the risks essential in the gaining of eternal life. The Bible suggests that while many are called into this humanizing relationship, very few actually are open to it. But the people of the Church continue to communicate the good news of their new humanity to all who will receive it. And they know that they could not carry out this mission without the strengthening of their humanness through the fellowship of the Church.

In addition to opposing the dehumanization that expresses itself between persons, the Church also opposes the dehumanization that results from the way many social institutions and political structures function in the modern world. When the government of South Africa dehumanizes its citizens through the practice of apartheid, the body of believers must not remain indifferent. When the Soviet Union and the United States pursue militaristic policies that threaten the survival of all of humanity, the Church must voice its opposition. When sexism is propagated in pornographic movies and magazines, the Church knows that it must strike back.

Hendrik Berkhof, in a very important book entitled *Christ and the Powers*, gives a brilliant exegesis of the Pauline expression "principalities and powers."[1] According to Berkhof, whenever the Apostle Paul uses the expression "principalities and powers," he is referring to any suprahuman forces or systems that exercise influence on human behavior. Berkhof contends that Paul makes it very clear that what we call social institutions are included among them. These principalities and powers, according to Berkhof, were created by God for the good of humanity. However, he points out that the Bible teaches that these principalities and powers have fallen under demonic control and are oppressing people rather than fulfilling their divine purposes. Having become bent on their own survival, they now exist to perpetuate themselves rather than to serve as instruments for humanization. People have been made to serve institutional ends rather than being served by institutions. Political, economic, and educational structures tend to become impersonal bureaucracies oriented toward efficiency rather than toward serving human interest. Having emerged *sui generis* from the interaction of people in society, social institutions have achieved an autonomy and a power that have potentialities for enslaving the very people whom they are intended to serve. In the words of Gordon Childe, once created, they have the capacity to recreate their creators. Emile Durkheim made a similar observation when he described societal institutions as "things" that are created by people, but gain the ability to constrain human behavior in a totalistic fashion.[2]

The dehumanizing tendencies inherent in social institutions have become increasingly clear. We are aware that there is a tendency toward tyranny in many social structures that are supposed to serve democratic ideals and human welfare. There are a host of essays and books that clearly demonstrate how political institutions can easily degenerate into impersonal bureaucracies that treat people as statistical entities rather than as persons. Most of us have been outraged by government that all too often diminishes our humanness by its refusal to treat us as persons.

It is easy to cite examples of the inhumane and depersonalized manner with which such bureaucracies relate to people, particularly in times of crisis. Recently I read a newspaper story about a man who took his son to the emergency ward of a hospital to be treated for acute appendicitis. While the boy cried and screamed in pain, the bureaucrats at the admissions desk required the father to fill out a variety of papers and then further delayed the treatment as they tried to ascertain which hospital plan would cover the expenses of the treatment. Finally the father grabbed the hospital administrator by the lapels of his coat, jerked him out of his seat, slammed him against the wall of the admissions office and said, "If you don't do something about my boy right now, I'm going to kill you." For this, the man was arrested and had to stand trial. In this case the procedures of the hospital had actually taken precedence over the well-being of the suffering child. The boy had cried and screamed for help, but nothing was done until the demands of the system had been satisfied. Ignoring the needs of persons, this system had become a demonic agent which dehumanized them.

Max Weber saw the threatening potentialities of bureaucracies, particularly in the field of economics. In his classic work *Social and Economic Organization*, he predicted that eventually bureaucratic institutions would prescribe human behavior so completely that man will be caged in by rules of his own making.[3] Eventually, says Weber, there will be an end to all human freedom, because all of life will be dictated by the demands of the social structure. Ultimately the social system will tell us what we can do and when we can do it. He argues that eventually no sector of life will be left to individual decision. Everything will be under the control of the system. Weber's description of the future is only an intellectualized statement predating more popular descriptions of what will happen to us, set forth by George Orwell and Aldous Huxley. These latter-day literary prophets have given us ample warnings of the eventual emergence of a government ruled by "Big Brother," and the kind of "brave new world" which lies ahead for us all.

It is in the face of such possibilities that the Apostle Paul admonishes us in Ephesians 6:12 to struggle against the principalities and powers. He, like these modern writers, saw that social systems created to serve the welfare of humanity tend to become autonomous systems oriented to their own self-preservation at the expense of the human spirit. Anticipating the scientific descriptions of Max Weber, Paul saw the necessity of exposing the demonic tendencies inherent in political and economic bureaucracies. He pointed out that on the cross Jesus exposed their true nature. Paul writes in the Epistle to the Colossians that the principalities and powers revealed their evil character when they plotted the death of Jesus. They claimed to be serving the interests of humanity and the cause of justice, but if that was true they would not have conspired to crucify the Son of God. The crucifixion of Jesus demonstrated the demonic tendencies inherent in social structures. At the trial of Jesus, the representatives of the religious and political systems of Israel declared that it was better for Jesus to be crucified than for the social system to which they were committed to be upset. What more evidence do we need to recognize what has happened to the principalities and powers?

The Bible clearly states that God is not against the principalities and powers, but rather is opposed to their tendency to usurp His lordship and to dominate the affairs of men. When they serve the interest of God, the principalities and powers are agents for good, creating the kind of order that allows for healthy social intercourse and human development. But when they slip away from the control of the Lord, they assume Godlike powers for themselves and become enemies of God and a curse to our humanity.

The Prophetic Implications of the 1960s Counterculture

Theodore Roszak, in his book *The Making of a Counter Culture*, sets forth the thesis that young people in the 1960s were rebelling against a social system they believed would make them into efficient servants in an enslaving society.[4] Their rebellion was a prophetic cry against totalitarian tendencies that have become the hallmark of many of the governments and economic systems of our modern age. By their actions, these young people assumed the role that I believe should have been played by the Church. Those of us who are part of the Body of Christ should have been the most committed opponents to the dehumanizing tendencies inherent in contemporary principalities and powers. However, we failed, and the prophets of the age turned out to be religiously cynical young people who did not know what else to do about the social system except to call for its destruction.

These anti-establishmentarians turned against the Church because they did not view it as a countervailing force against

the tendencies toward dehumanization manifested in political
and economic structures. Instead they viewed the Church as a
legitimator of those oppressive institutions, sanctifying their
evil practices and even calling these structures sacred. They
saw that in reality the Church had become just one more of the
principalities and powers from which humanity needed liberation. When the Church failed to speak out against the demonic qualities of the principalities and powers, I believe that God
chose to use other means for expressing His outrage against
their dehumanizing tendencies. Consequently, the long-haired
counterculture young people dressed in jeans and khaki jack-
ets became His instruments for challenging the works of Sa-
tan. They carried the banners of protest that should have been
carried by those of us who call ourselves Christians.

The voices of protest that marked the '60s have been silenced. Young people today seldom rage against the establish-
ment that they once deemed "fascist" or oppressive. Instead
they now opt for jobs in the very social institutions they once
condemned. They have cut their hair, put on three-piece suits,
and taken up attaché cases. There seems to be no one left to
decry the abuses of the principalities and powers.

It is easy to see, in the light of these recent developments,
that the Church has an opportunity to reassert its prophetic
role. The world needs a Church that will struggle against the
principalities and powers and call them into conformity with
the will of God. The Body of Christ has a new opportunity to
lead the struggle against practices or tendencies inherent in
contemporary social structures that would prevent the humanization, and hence the salvation, of God's people. If a mul-
tinational corporation should exploit the people of some Third
World country, ripping off its natural resources, and under-
paying employees, while producing products that in no way
meet the desperate needs of the native population, the Church
must respond and seek to liberate the people from these forms
of oppression. If the schools of some large city graduate students who are functional illiterates and therefore unable to

function with dignity as employable adults, Christians, who have been humanized by the resurrected Christ, must champion programs to change these schools. If the government is controlled by special interest groups that are able to influence congressmen and senators to serve their own interests in opposition to the public good, then the Church must be ready to speak out against such manipulation and work to make government more responsive to the needs of citizens.

The Effectiveness of Authority

It seems to me that if the Church is going to effect change in society without betraying its claim to be the Body of Christ, it must abandon the use of *power*. Instead, the church must rely on *authority*. Power is the ability to force people to do your will even against their own. Authority is the ability to elicit the cooperation of people who want to do your will out of a sense of love or duty.

It is quite obvious that when Jesus sought to change the world He did so through the use of authority. When He entered history two thousand years ago, He abandoned power and came in the weakness of human flesh. The second chapter of Philippians tells us, He who "thought it not robbery to be equal with God . . . emptied Himself and took upon Himself the form of a slave, making Himself of no reputation and humbling Himself even to death, even the death of the cross." When Jesus entered history He did not come with the pomp and glory of a Caesar. He did not depend on the support of an army. He did not operate from a position of wealth. Instead He became what the prophet Isaiah called "the suffering servant."

Jesus did not come with the kind of power that this world understands. But when He spoke, He spoke with authority and many people listened to Him. Since His day, untold millions have followed Him, *choosing* to do His will rather than being forced into it. His authority has been built on sacrificial love, manifested and expressed in the crucifixion. Referring to His death on the cross, He said, "If I be lifted up, I will draw all men unto myself" (John 12:32). He believed that if you love other people so much that you are willing to suffer in order that they might experience good, they will eventually respond to you and acknowledge your authority.

The style used by Jesus for bringing about social change provides one reason I find myself at odds with the movement in America that has come to be known as the Moral Majority. I find myself troubled that the people of that group seek to use power to effect social change. They mobilize public opinion in order to threaten congressmen, senators, and even the President. They have learned to brag about their ability to drive people from office, claiming that they have the power to restructure America in accord with their own designs. Their exercise of power often enforces conformity, but it inevitably breeds resentment, and therefore destroys the possibilities for the kind of humanizing love that characterizes the presence of Jesus.

Whenever the Church has aligned itself with political power, it has experienced extreme corruption. When Emperor Constantine issued the Edict of Milan, making Christianity the official religion of the empire, he did more to destroy Christianity than did all the Caesars who sought to extinguish the Church by throwing Christians to the lions. When, under Constantine, the Church became aligned with political power, it betrayed the style of its founder, and committed itself to a pattern of decay. Having failed to learn this lesson from history, the Moral Majority is likely to repeat this mistake of the past, as it probably will gain more power in the years to come. But the more it gains power, the more it will lose authority. People throughout the nation, and perhaps throughout the world, who may be forced to accept its dictates, consequently may be hardened against the Christ whom the Moral Majority sincerely desires to communicate.

There are many who would argue that without power, society cannot be changed. As notable a person as Reinhold

Niebuhr has argued that while power corrupts the people of God, they must of necessity assume power in order to do good. Niebuhr was aware that when Christians gain a political office or use military force in order to bring about social justice, they find themselves in morally ambiguous positions. However, Niebuhr feels that there is no alternative to such an option. He believes that Christians must either use power themselves or allow the world to be victimized by less benevolent persons who will. I do not agree. I think there is ample evidence that positive social change can be brought about without the use of power.

Looking at the Evidence

I believe that Mother Teresa is a person who has no power, but a great deal of authority. It was interesting to observe her role in a recent Middle East crisis. She was able to talk to heads of governments and to lead them into more peaceful courses of action. They listened to her, not because she had power, but because she had authority established through her sacrificial service to humanity.

Another example of the effectiveness of authority can be cited in the style of leadership employed by Martin Luther King. Many of us will remember the day King led his followers out of Salem, Alabama, on a "Freedom March" to the state capital. He made sure that all who participated in the march went through a long period of prayer and spiritual purging so that they might be rid of any resentment against their oppressors. He psychologically prepared them to endure persecution, and if need be, martyrdom. They solemnly marched out of Selma and shortly thereafter confronted an array of angry policemen and deputy sheriffs on a bridge just outside the town. When told to turn back, King responded, "We have come too far to turn back now." He and his fellow marchers got down on their knees and bowed their heads in prayer. The police and the deputy sheriffs ran towards them, their billy clubs in the air. Heads were bashed, blood was shed, and the Civil Rights demonstrators were left sprawled all over the road.

The whole scene was captured on live television and broadcast from one end of America to another. I, along with millions of others, saw it all happen. And as I watched that scene on television, something inside of me said, "They've won! King and his followers have won! The Civil Rights movement is victorious!" I knew in the strange economy of God the losers had become the winners and the winners had become the losers. The Civil Rights movement had triumphed, not because of lawsuits, boycotts, and pressure tactics; it had won because King and his followers were willing to be crucified for their cause. Their suffering had effected political change.

Martin Luther King had learned his Bible lessons well. He knew that triumph belongs to those who love their enemies and are willing to be spitefully abused by those who hate them. He realized that the way of Christ was the only way in which racism could be effectively challenged. King understood that the oppressor needed deliverance as much as the oppressed. He realized that racial discrimination not only dehumanizes the suffering minority, but it destroys the humanity of the domineering racist. Both need to be delivered by humanizing love. That is what Jesus taught and that is what King tried to live. He knew that even in the oppressive enemy Jesus waited to be loved.

The means the Church uses to change social institutions into instruments that foster humanization must be carefully selected. Nietzsche once said, "Be careful when you fight the dragon lest you become a dragon." That warning is important to heed. Too often, in an effort to bring about social justice, crusaders dehumanize those people who would oppose their aims and goals. Those who champion the cause of the poor can easily come to regard the rich as selfish creatures lacking any kind of feeling or sense of justice. It is always easier to paint the opponent as the devil and refuse to see that he too is loved by

God and incarnates the sacred presence of the Eternal Thou. In an attempt to set the world right the Church often justifies the use of violence and acts out of a sense of vengeance. Those who are rich and those who are powerful exploiters sometimes come to be regarded by Christian reformers as "things" that must be destroyed rather than persons to be loved.

A Warning from Mission Impossible: This Message Will Self-Destruct

There are some warnings that I wish to issue to anyone reading this book. The first is to be aware that the theology expressed in this short volume represents a personal attempt to state my Christian faith in a way that might prove meaningful for my secularist friends. I am sensitive to the fact that any attempt to state the Gospel in the dominant categories of a culture inevitably leads to a distortion of that Gospel. Consequently, anyone who accuses me of violating the biblical message is correct. I know that the Gospel is infinitely more than these few limited statements jotted down for your consideration.

In some respects my theology, like *any* theology, is heresy, if by heresy we mean a presentation of God's message that is incomplete, inadequate, and potentially dangerous. However, what can be said about what I have done can also be said, perhaps to a much lesser degree, about what was done in other stages of social-historical development by Luther, Calvin,

Zwingli, and Wesley. Anyone who endeavors to theologize for the people of his culture is guilty of missing important dimensions of the whole truth of God. Every theologian understates some biblical truths and misunderstands others. All who attempt to contextualize theology and express God's message within the limited boundaries of their respective cultural systems realize that they "know in part and prophesy in part" and are aware that "when that which is perfect is come then that which is in part shall be done away." Furthermore, even if what I have written makes sense now, I realize that the cultural milieu will change, a new world-view will emerge and my statements will be rendered meaningless, even if they do have some meaning now.

I believe the Bible to be an infallible message from God, but I also believe that it remains a task for men and women in each new culture to express that biblical message in ways they think might be relevant to their contemporaries. I am convinced that one of the worst uses of the theologies of the reformers is to treat them as though they are final authoritative interpretations of the biblical message, applicable to all people in all places at all times. Theologies come and theologies go. They briefly speak to the people of their times and then pass into insignificance, being replaced by new attempts to state the ineffable message of God. Truly, "we have this truth in earthen vessels." The old vessels tend to break, and every society seeks new vessels to carry the truth for its people.

At best a theology points people to Jesus. It is not the truth, but it points people to the truth. When the truth is known, it will prove to be so much more than the theological expression of it that the theology will come to be regarded as foolishness (1 Cor. 3:19). I do not want anyone to put his faith in my words, but I invite everyone to put his faith in my Christ. Somehow, when the Gospel is preached it converts people, not because preachers set it forth with perfection or accuracy, but because the Holy Spirit helps the hearer of the Gospel to discern its meaning. Somehow, the person of Christ breaks through the written and spoken words of preachers and theologians and is experienced in power and truth by those who are willing to receive Him. In the end, the best I can offer is the assurance that I have tried to be faithful to Scripture and did not deliberately misconstrue its message.

Second, in describing the resurrected Jesus as the sacred presence waiting to be encountered in other people, I was making a literal statement. I do *not* mean that others *represent* Jesus for us. I mean that Jesus *actually* is *present* in each other person. He continues to live in our midst, *not* as a religious influence or a sacred idea—He is personally alive. It is the historical Jesus who is encountered in the "I-Thou." It is the resurrected Lord of the universe who is revealed to those who are open to His presence in others. Jesus is a real presence in other people, and this convinces me that there are infinite possibilities for the future and great hope for the world. Jesus is alive in the world working through people who yield to His leading. He is moving people towards oneness. He is bringing them together as the Body of Christ. His presence is evidence that the Kingdom of God is among us.

I have come to my convictions about where Jesus can be found through personal discoveries. I say that Jesus can be found in others because I have found Him there. While looking into the eyes of certain persons, I have realized that they were entrances to the holy of holies where God waited to be loved. Human encounters have made me an heir to the grace of God. Special people have touched my life in such a way that, afterwards, I realized that I had been touched by Jesus. Such experiences have proven to be revelations through which the Eternal God has broken into my life and has taken the deadness of my soul away. I am speaking of encounters with a personal God, not merely good feelings that follow pleasant times with special people.

Theology, like good fiction, is always biographical. It is more likely to describe the experiences and reflections of the author than the ultimate truth about things. Consequently, I have written of a God that I myself have come to know and respond to in the flesh. When I encountered Him hidden behind the personhood of others I was fortunate enough to recognize Him for who He is.

Lastly, I am convinced that real theology can only be developed in praxis. Only by trying to love people and serve them in their needs can knowledge of God be gleaned. The frustrations, sufferings, joys, sorrows, and depressions that accompany attempts to do something of value for others are what force us to look for meaning in what we do and for significance in the people we serve. Our quest for ultimate value sometimes leads nowhere, and we are left with a sense of futility and wonder why we even bothered. However, there are other times—rare to be sure—when we realize we have walked and talked with Jesus and have served some sublime purpose. He usually overtakes us as a stranger we meet on the road. Our hearts burn within as we talk with Him, and afterward we know that we have entertained the Lord.

Notes

Chapter 1

1. *The Positive Philosophy of August Comte,* freely translated and condensed by Harriet Martineau, vol. 3 (London: Bell, 1896), pp. 305–8.
2. Karl Marx, selected writings in *Sociology and Social Philosophy,* trans. T. B. Bottomore (New York: McGraw-Hill, 1964).
3. Henry Steele Commager, *The American Mind* (New Haven, CT: Yale University Press, 1950), chap. 4; Robert A. Nisbet, *The Sociological Tradition* (New York: Basic Books, 1966), chap. 2; Kenneth Bock, "Theories of Progress, Development, Evolution," in *A History of Sociological Analysis,* ed. T. Bottomore and Robert Nisbet (New York: Basic Books, 1978), chap. 2.
4. Calvin S. Hall, *A Primer of Freudian Psychology* (New York: New American Library), chap. 2.
5. Sigmund Freud, *Civilization and Its Discontents* (New York: Norton, 1961).
6. Janko Larrin, *Nietszche* (New York: Charles Scribner's Sons, 1971).
7. R. P. Cuzzort, *Humanity and Modern Sociological Thought* (New York: Holt, Rinehart and Winston, 1969), chap. 9.
8. A. Flew and A. MacIntyre, eds., *New Essays in Philosophical Theology* (London: SCM Press, 1955), pp. 96 f.

Chapter 2

1. Julien Freund, *The Sociology of Max Weber* (New York: Vintage Books), pp. 3–36.
2. Karl Heim, *Christian Faith and Natural Science*, trans. N. Horton Smith (New York: Harper and Bros., 1957).
3. Bryan Wilson, *Religion in Secular Society* (Baltimore: Penguin Books, 1966).
4. Ibid., pp. 43, 64–66.
5. Robert K. Merton, *Social Theory and Social Structure* (New York: Free Press, 1968), chap. 20.
6. Langdon Gilkey, *Naming the Whirlwind* (New York: Bobbs-Merril Co., 1969), pp. 39–71.

Chapter 3

1. Commager, *The American Mind*, chap. 4.
2. Will Durant, *The Story of Philosophy* (Garden City, NY: Garden City Publishing Co., 1943), pp. 301 ff.
3. Richard Bach, *Jonathan Livingston Seagull* (New York: Macmillan, 1970).
4. Vernon Sproxton, *Teilhard de Chardin* (London: SCM Press, 1971); Pierre Teilhard de Chardin, *The Phenomenon of Man* (New York: Harper and Row, 1959).
5. John T. Robinson, *Honest to God* (Philadelphia: Westminster Press, 1963), pp. 13–14.
6. Alexandre Koyré, *From the Closed World to the Infinite Universe* (New York: Harper and Bros., 1957), chaps. 2 and 3.
7. See Lincoln Barnett, *The Universe and Dr. Einstein* (New York: Mentor Books, 1963).
8. Sir Arthur Eddington, *The Expanding Universe* (Ann Arbor, MI: Ann Arbor Paperbacks, 1958), p. 13.
9. Edward G. Kuhlman, "A Christian Interpretation of Humanity for Social Work," an unpublished dissertation prepared for the School of Social Work at the University of Pennsylvania (1982), provides an excellent review of the debate over the behaviorist model.
10. B. F. Skinner, *Beyond Freedom and Dignity* (New York: Bantam Books, 1971).
11. Ibid., pp. 191–92.

12. An article by Alan Dawe, "Theories of Social Action," in *A History of Sociological Analysis*, ed. Tom Bottomore and Robert Nisbet, pp. 362–417, and a book by Roscoe C. Hinkle, Jr., and Gisela J. Hinkle, *The Development of Modern Sociology* (New York: Random House, 1960), provide good surveys of social action thought.

13. See Gila J. Hayim, *The Existential Sociology of Jean-Paul Sartre* (Amherst, MA: University of Massachusetts Press, 1980).

14. See George Herbert Mead, *Mind, Self and Society*, vol. 1 (Chicago: University of Chicago Press, 1934), chaps. 2 and 3.

15. Viktor Emil Frankl, *Man's Search for Meaning: An Introduction to Logotherapy* (Boston: Beacon Press, 1962).

16. Martin Heidegger, *Existence and Being* (Chicago: Henry Regnery, 1960).

17. Charles M. Sheldon, *In His Steps* (Nashville: Broadman Press, 1935).

18. A brilliant example of the contemporary use of Freud's theories is Philip Rieff's *Freud: The Mind of the Moralist* (New York: Viking Press, 1959).

19. See F. Barron and T. Leary, "Changes in Psychoneurotic Patients with and without Psychotherapy," *Journal of Counseling Psychology* 19 (1955).

20. Sigmund Freud, *Civilization and Its Discontents* (New York: W. W. Norton, 1961), pp. 91 f.

21. Peter Berger and Thomas Luckmann, *The Social Construction of Reality* (New York: Anchor Books, 1967), pp. 157–61, 169–70.

Chapter 4

1. A biographical introduction to Sartre is provided by Philip Thody, *Sartre* (New York: Charles Scribner's Sons, 1971).

2. See Sigmund Freud, *Totem and Taboo* (New York: Norton, 1950), and Emile Durkheim, *The Elementary Forms of the Religious Life*, trans. Joseph Ward Swain (New York: Free Press, 1965). See also Sigmund Freud, *The Future of an Illusion* (New York: Norton, 1961).

3. Søren Kierkegaard, *The Point of View for My Work as an Author*, trans. Walter Lowrie, and Walter Lowrie, *A Short Life of Søren Kierkegaard* (New York: Anchor Books, 1961). Also see Søren Kierkegaard, *Concluding Unscientific Postscript*, trans. David F. Swenson and Walter Lowrie (Princeton: Princeton University Press, 1941), pp. 96 ff., 262ff

Chapter 5

1. An excellent intellectual biography of Blaise Pascal is Emile Cailliet's *Pascal: The Emergence of Genius* (New York: Harper Torchbooks, 1945).
2. See Elizabeth Kübler-Ross, *On Death and Dying* (New York: Macmillan, 1969).
3. See Gail Sheehy, *Passages* (New York: Bantam Books, 1977).
4. Martin Heidegger, *Sein und Zeit* (Halle, Germany: 1927), pp. 187–256.
5. Thornton Wilder, *Our Town* (New York: Coward McCann, 1938).
6. See Martin Buber, *I and Thou*, trans. Walter Kaufmann (New York: Charles Scribner's Sons, 1970).
7. The lecture notes of Mead were published in 3 volumes, George Herbert Mead, *Mind, Self and Society*, ed. Charles W. Morris (Chicago: University of Chicago Press, 1934).
8. The development of these ideas was the result of reading Maurice Natanson, *The Journeying Self* (Reading, MA: Addison-Wesley Publishing Co., 1970), chaps. 1 and 2.
9. For an excellent review of Buber's life and works, see Maurice S. Friedman, *Martin Buber: The Life of Dialogue* (Chicago: University of Chicago Press, 1955).
10. *Augustine, The Confessions*, trans. Edward B. Pusey (New York: Pocket Books, 1951), XI, p. 14.
11. Immanuel Kant, *Critique of Pure Reason*, abr. and trans. Norman Kemp Smith (New York: Random House, 1958), pp. A31–A36.
12. Lincoln Barnett, *The Universe and Dr. Einstein*, pp. 39–41.
13. James A. Coleman, *Relativity for the Layman* (New York: New American Library, 1959), pp. 65–73.
14. For an appraisal of the work of Paul Tillich, see *The Theology of Paul Tillich*, ed. Charles W. Kegley and Robert W. Bretall (New York: Macmillan, 1961).

Chapter 6

1. See Thomas Hobbes, *Leviathan* (New York: G. P. Putnam's Sons, 1904).
2. See William Graham Sumner, *Folkways: A Study of the Sociological Importance of Usages, Manners, Customs, Mores, and Morals* (Boston: Ginn, 1940).

3. See Margaret Mead, *Coming of Age in Samoa* (New York: William Morrow, 1928).

4. See Bronislaw Malinowski, *The Sexual Life of Savages in Northwestern Melanesia: An Ethnographic Account of Courtship, Marriage and Family Life among the Natives of the Trobriand Islands, British New Guinea* (New York: Harcourt, Brace and World, 1929).

5. *New York Times*, December 23, 1952; also see Paul Hutchinson, "The President's Religious Faith," *The Christian Century*, March 24, 1954.

6. See Henri Lefebvre, *The Sociology of Marx* (New York: Random House, Vintage Books, 1968), chap. 3.

7. See Karl Mannheim, *Ideology and Utopia* (London: Routledge and Kegan Paul, 1936).

8. See Max Scheler, *Versuche zu einer Soziologie des Wissens* (Tübingen: Niemeyer, 1924).

9. See Ronald Sider, *Rich Christians in an Age of Hunger* (Downers Grove, IL: Inter-Varsity Press, 1977).

10. See Jose Miquez Bonino, *Doing Theology in a Revolutionary Situation* (Philadelphia: Fortress Press, 1975).

11. See Rubem Alves, *A Theology of Human Hope* (Washington: Corpus Books, 1969).

12. See Juan Luis Segundo, *The Community Called Church* (Maryknoll, NY: Orbis Books, 1972).

13. See Camilo Torres, *Revolutionary Priest: The Complete Writings and Messages of Camilo Torres*, ed. Hohn Gerassi (New York: Random House, Vintage Books, 1971).

14. See Gustavo Gutierrez, *A Theology of Liberation* (Maryknoll, NY: Orbis Books, 1973).

15. See James Cone, *A Black Theology of Liberation* (Philadelphia: Lippincott, 1970).

16. For a summary of Barth's view of Scripture, see David L. Mueller, *Karl Barth* (Waco, TX: Word Books, 1972), pp. 56–59. See also Langdon Gilkey, *Naming the Whirlwind*, pp. 82–87.

17. See William Hamilton, *The New Essence of Christianity* (New York: Association Press, 1961). See also Gilkey, *Naming the Whirlwind*, pp. 115–124.

18. See A. H. Maslow, *The Further Reaches of Human Nature* (New York: Viking Press, 1971); see also A. H. Maslow, *Toward a Psychology of Being*, 2nd ed. (Princeton: Van Nostrand, 1968).

19. See Erich Fromm, *The Art of Loving* (New York: Harper, Colophon Books, 1956).

Chapter 7

1. Paul Tillich, *Systematic Theology*, vol. 1 (Chicago: University of Chicago Press, 1951), pp. 8–11.
2. Martin Buber, *I and Thou*, p. 62.

Chapter 8

1. See Hendrik Berkhof, *Christ and the Powers*, trans. John H. Yoder (Scottdale, PA: Herald Press, 1962).
2. Emile Durkheim, *The Rules of the Sociological Method* (New York: Free Press, 1964), pp. 1–13.
3. Max Weber, *The Theory of Social and Economic Organization*, trans. A. M. Henderson and Talcott Parson (New York: Free Press, 1947), pp. 363–73; also see *From Max Weber*, ed. and trans. H. H. Gerth and C. Wright Mills (New York: Oxford University Press, 1946), chap. 8. An excellent statement on Weber's concept of rationalization is found in Julien Freund, *The Sociology of Max Weber*, pp. 17–24.
4. See Theodore Roszak, *The Making of a Counter Culture* (Garden City, NY: Anchor Books, 1968).

THE DREAM
Keith Miller

In the Dream, Keith Miller invites us to go on an imaginative journey with him to try to look at ourselves and the church the way God might look at us.

It is not always a happy journey. In many ways, the story shows, we in God's church have let Him down – failing to love and forgive one another, by failing to reach outside ourselves and help those who are in need.

The book is pervaded with a sense of the Lord's sadness and righteous anger over these sins. But it also shines with His overwhelming love, concern and forgiveness. It is fundamentally, a book of hope.

ISBN 0-85009-061-X

YOU CAN MAKE A DIFFERENCE
Tony Campolo

This book challenges young people to make their lives count for Christ. Tony Campolo uniquely identifies with young people in their own situation, then shows how they can use the power of God to change their world. With his incomparable blend of humour and serious biblical insights, the author deals with commitment, vocation, dating and discipleship.

ISBN 0-85009-056-3

PRAYER: KEY TO REVIVAL
Paul Y Cho with R. Whitney Manzano

The secret behind the growth of the largest church in the world!

'No man can schedule a revival', Dr Cho has said, 'for God alone is the giver of life. But . . . when 'the fullness of time' is come and prayer ascends from a few earnest hearts, then history teaches it is time for the tide of revival to sweep in once more.'

This perspective is born of Dr Cho's conviction that while revival is the sovereign work of the Holy Spirit, the earnest prayers of God's people must work with the Spirit. It is then that He moves anew in the hearts of unbelievers.

ISBN 0-85009-059-8

PRESENTING

TONY CAMPOLO ON VIDEO

YOU CAN MAKE A DIFFERENCE
A FOUR-PART SERIES FOR YOUTH

1 Commitment
Getting Beyond Good Intentions

"It is what we commit ourselves to that gives us identity, meaning and purpose in life, and commitment to Christ is the only commitment of lasting value."

2 Vocation
Setting the course and travelling light

"We have a responsibility to be in the places where we are most desperately needed . . . do something great for Jesus. The time has come for a whole new generation."

3 Dating
Turning your love life over to Jesus

"Spiritually is caring for people who are hurting . . . reach out to the kid who is left out and make him feel included – give Christian love."

4 Discipleship
Living life to the nth degree

"Study the Bible and get to know the Author. Set aside time to be inwardly still; to hear the voice of God. Get involved with a support group – you are empowered through fellowship. You need the Church and the Church desperately needs you."

YOU CAN MAKE A DIFFERENCE videos are just some of over 20 videos currently available from Word (UK).

Word Publishing
Word (UK) Ltd
9 Holdom Avenue, Bletchley,
Milton Keynes, MK1 1QU